Going

THE

Distance

WITH

Jimmy Howe

JIMMY HOWE

First published 2018
By TaigaTales

Cover Designed By Lauren Howe

All videos to accompany this story are found on YouTube... Simply punch in:
jimmy howe – GoingTheDistance – OutInAfrica

The videos are just a little extra from the journey for your enjoyment.
I will endeavor to keep all videos on the channel for the foreseeable future,
however, check out the FaceBook page for any updates. You just never know...
Find Us...GoingTheDistance on FaceBook...

Alternatively email me jimmyhowertw@icloud.com and I'll tell you where to go...
providing I have internet connection.

Acknowledgements

To say it's wasn't easy for me to put pen to paper is an understatement.
For those of you who know me maybe it is easy to understand.
I stuttered, I faltered, Hey I was lost at times. Imagine a dyslexic Scotsman
floundering around St. Petersburg with a dodgy Russian road map and you'll be
someway there to understanding. As then, I simple asked them who knew.

There is an endless list of friends and acquaintances from the road, who will always
bring a smile to my face when the wheels stop turning. There was a few who were
less than welcoming shall we say... It just is what it is... Hey I'll just notch them up to
experience as the good far outweighed the bad.

I must thank Rae for encouraging me oh so much in the writing of my tale and for
sorting out my spelling. I'm sure he doesn't need to imagine lost boy with a dodgy
map. My command of the English language must have brought a smile to his face
many a time. My daughter Lauren for designing the book cover, thanks Tinker and
Karl for helping me to pull it all together. A Diamond Geezer. Thanks to my mate
Jock for putting up with me and Alan & Lorraine for keeping my feet on the ground
when my heid was in the clouds. A Big thanks to my family for their support, just
nice to know they are there for you I suppose.

...Thanks to you for GoingThe Distance... *Jimmy*

Below Space
On the Earth, on Bikes
Through water, sand and dirt tracks
We have travelled
In our journey spanning many miles
This story will be unravelled

Ladies and Gentlemen

The story you are about to read is true...Well...most of it...
But in those immortal words from *Dragnet*...
Only the names have changed to protect the...not so Innocent...

Leaving The Marines with a box of CD's, a bag full of T-shirts and
a bicycle, Jimmy thought his days of traveling the globe were over.
20 years later, how his world has changed! He has a motorbike
and a bag with a few less T-shirts…but
Hey he's still smiling…

Contents

Long Distance Relationship

Dinner for two over the iPad as there are 400 miles between us. I'm not sure if it's what Steve Jobs had in mind for his creation but it served a purpose. It allowed us to carry on and develop a long distance relationship. I was in Scotland and the Trick-Cyclist in England.

We'd sit on an evening chatting over dinner through FaceTime about our hopes and dreams. Since Heidi had come to Scotland the year before we had been as thick as thieves, scheming and dreaming of the road. We would travel the length of the country to be in each others company when we could, but when at work this was the best we could do.

Maybe it was easier over the ether as we asked many a searching question of each other. Questions we might not have asked if we were face to face in real time. She'd ask me questions of my times in the Royal Marines. The good, the bad and the outrageous. Stories from the Jungles of Borneo, the flea infestation in Northern Iraq and absolute hell of training in Egypt. Tell me something Juicy she would ask.

I think she was stunned when I told her I'd been deported from Turkey. WTF? Just a misunderstanding, Honest!

She would tell me of the stories peddling, paddling and back-packing around the world. Life on the road as a single female traveller, to the juicy stuff from her trip through Africa that just couldn't be printed in the book she had written. Her parents, her family and the rest of the world didn't need to know everything she'd say with a smile. There has to be a little mystique. I suppose she's right.

1

Hey if we were gonna be with each other this was real enough. Oh, there was plenty humdrum of everyday life. The kind of thing that makes you dream even more of making that escape. Dreams of hitting the road…

Glass of wine in hand it was all so easy…What's your favourite film? In Bruges… "It's a Fucking Fairy Tale" …We had a starting point.

I'd like to go to Waterloo…Maybe hiking in the Alps…

Tour Mount Blanc? We had a general direction.

A guy in the TRF (Trail Riders Federation) gave me GPS tracks for Albania and the Balkans. We could get a ferry to Africa from there maybe? Wow! plans for OutInAfrica…

The Crazy-one has always had plans for Africa. Me? I just can't believe it… but I'm all in…

It wasn't all down to the wine, but before we knew it we had plans from Euro-Hike to OutInAfrica taking shape! Plans? Well a vague line across the map. We'd both been on longer journeys which had been researched and meticulously planned. Just not sure if that rigid plan is always the way forward. Let's just see what happens…

It's just the case of getting out the door then, and that one we had both done before… Bruges… "It's a Fucking Fairytale"… Africa? See you in my Dreams… No?

Does Yir Arse Fit Ye ... Jimmy's Journal...

Mongolian summer of 2013, riding a Triumph Tiger 800XC

Got to keep on rolling. The GS guys were brilliant. A German and two Swiss guys travelling on the oversized BMW GS motorbike. They helped me out and slowed me down. Settled me into the Mongolian way of things. Well until I smashed the bike for a second time.

The first time was bad enough it had reminded me about being out here on my own. It never really bothered me until here. Yeah yeah being on your own you have to be aware of your surroundings that bit more I feel. But trapped under your bike with no one around. Just doesn't bear thinking about!

I had the sleepless nights at home dreaming of the bears and wolfs in the Siberian Taiga.

To be Honest I watched the film **The Grey** with Liam Neeson. Big wolf story where the survivors of a plane crash out in Alaska where being systematical hunted down by the wolf pack.

Not quite the same but it led to many a night thinking of being eaten by the wolf as a lay trapped under my bike somewhere alone in the forest. The scary picture of my bike being found with a single boot trapped under it and the lower part of my leg still inside.

Oh so glad I met them as I run out of talent. Face down in the dirt with the tiger on top of me. Probably caused by the Tiger running so badly to be honest. Riding the revs and slipping the clutch to keep it

3

running I went into things just a little hot shall we say. Bent it a bit more and broke off the front brake. But who needs that out here? Pity as the rear had stopped working a while back. Calliper piston had seized. Keep on rolling, I'm sure I'll get there. It was more the broken wrist I was worried about. The GS guys had picked the bike up off me and straightened me out. Didn't stop me bubbling inside me helmet for the next 20km or so. Bugga!

Thankfully the wrist turned out just to be badly bruised. I was struggling but I would manage with the help of my new friends. That just might have been End-Ex

Being trapped under the bike was the stuff of nightmares...

Night-time visitors were nearly always welcome. Chit-chat and an exchange of gifts was always good. Something of a tradition here. One in particular stands out in The Okan Valley. So far off the beaten track that I'm sure not many Overlanders came by this way.

The side of the river with the Yurt or Ger camp near by. A Mongolian round house of old, preferred by the nomadic herders out here. Something that had stood the test of time since the days of Genghis Khan and before. Something that's so easy and versatile, suited to their nomadic lifestyle. The Mongolian people caught onto Glamping long before we did.

Yip, over he came but he was only concerned about the grazing for his livestock. We can move but he stayed for a while to chat. Well, the best we could. Off he went after a while and left us to it, returning later in the evening with his kids. One in his arms and the other in hand.

Exchange of gifts. He gave us Airag or Eric as it sounded to me and the by now dreaded cheese sticks. It kinda reminded me of an alcoholic macrobiotic drink but not in a good way. The Eric that is not the cheese sticks. They're just rank rotten! I made him coffee with a dash of Sailor Jerry (Spiced Rum), but I know who got the better deal (and it wasn't me). Haribo and chocolate for the kids. Oh! I had to take the lollipop back off the little one as she tried to eat it with the wrapper still on.

Mmm... not sure she ever had one of these before.

Beautiful night but something a little surreal. Two Swiss, a German, a Scotsman and now a native Mongolian goat herder sitting under the stars. Chewing the fat and drinking this strange brew supplied by his mare, fermented in a sheep's stomach. Yeah tried not to think about that bit. But being a Scotsman I've eaten Haggis all my life, you think I'd be used to that one. The Haggis not fermented in the sheep's stomach but it's been laced with the good stuff (whisky) in the past.

Yet another night-time visitor. Never sure what it really was but just as I went for the zipper of the tent I heard the commotion outside. Shit! I'm not going out there. Don't need to pee that badly. The dogs from the Ger camp going ballistic, right outside me tent. Then the next encampment up the valley and the next by the time I've got me riding gear back on and helmet in hand. I was Well Spooked! Definitely not going out there!

Took me a lifetime to drop off to sleep with my bike gear on. Hey! in my head I thought it protect me.

In the morning. Tracks up the edge of the riverbank suggested something I'd rather not think about. And as we chatted to our new neighbour there was a few raised eyebrows. Wolf!

Bugger! Pack up and go!! Another hard day's ride to Tsetserlegs.

The Fairfield Guesthouse

Probably what I'd been waiting for. Cappuccino and a good bed.

Awesome. The simple things in life!!

Blonde hair curves. Mmm! Things are looking up!!

Met a crazy cycling chic. She was on her push bike traveling in the other direction. Never felt so inadequate as I tried to give her advice of the road that lay ahead for her. A more experienced traveller I'll never meet. She had taken 2 years to cycle to Cape Town and countless other trips.

You couldn't buy me a ticket to take me to Africa! As I shared my only African experience with her. Egypt! Three weeks of hell whilst I was in The Marines...

As I chatted to her I realised I had met her before. I know you!

When I had left home I went to a Horizons Unlimited Overlanders gathering in Donnington. I remembered some of her story. She was a girl that had sat next to me in a Russian Discussion group.

Never forget a set of curves!

Can remember checking her out as she wiggled away that day. Never in my wildest dreams did I imagine I'd meet her ever again, never! Certainly never out here. Small world eh!

Probably the most intriguing girl I'll ever meet.

A visit to the local Nadam Festival with the crazy chic, just hope this wasn't the last time we met… in my dreams I often punch above my weight.

Hey we can all dream…

A couple of nights and the push for the capital. But hey we have time. This is Mongolia after all, my friend!

Wrestling, horseback racing and archery. All the skills of a warrior nation.

A visit to Erdinazu Monastery. A peaceful place in where Genghis Khan supposedly ruled from. Hard to say as they were and still are a mostly nomadic people.

A night in the sand dunes and the road to Ulaanbaatar. Mongol Els Ger Camp.

I've been in bigger more crowded cities than this but never one with more chaos! Just Chaos!

A city that's trying to run before it can walk. Terrible infrastructure! Holes in the road everywhere and traffic chaos. It was the same back in Tsetserlect. The people have never grown up with the modern day traffic that we've become accustomed to. They've never had to learn so they don't understand the simple code of the road. Pass and overtake for the sake of it. Doesn't matter that no one is going anywhere they'll just overtake. Just bizarre! Wrong side of the road? Not here its empty I can use it surely! More bizarre!

The sanity of the Oasis. A biker friendly guesthouse and Ger

Camp. This is the place I was heading for. Almost all Overlanders head here. Bikers, 4x4 Drivers and Unimog Pilots of all nationalities. That makes it sound like thousands but still only about 20 or so. Can't believe I had become one of them. But I suppose I had!

A friendly place for exchange of information. Of which I was in need. Wasn't sure of my next move with the sickly Tiger. Siberia was not the place for it and I need to work out my options.

I had already contacted Triumph hoping for some help but they weren't interested. We'd need to plug it into the computer. Yeah like I can take it down the local dealership. The nearest one was in Tokyo. Mmm…

Skeleton Coast
Orupembe
Oshakati
Opuwo

NAMIBIA

Swakopmund
Walvis Bay
Windhoek
Solitaire

BOTSWANA

Gaborone

Nelspruit

Swaziland

LESOTHO

SOUTH
AFRICA

Sani
Pass

Hogsback

Cederberg
Baviaanskloof
Capetown
Port
Elizabeth

Cape Agulhas

Map No. 1

1
Out In Africa

Africa was a reality

South Africa was a reality and we can pick up our bikes in the morning.

Reality? Wow, never thought I'd ever be here. A Month of Sunday's my maw would say.

Exhausted and hotter than hell. It had been a long haul from Heathrow to Cape Town.

Hostel life for a few days to sort ourselves out and we can hit the road. Bikes first though.

Our European tour had come to an end back in Bulgaria. Seemed the correct thing to do at the time. Go home sort the Bikes out and ship them to Cape Town. The Mediterranean Migrants Crisis was really coming to a head. We were struggling to find a ferry to Egypt, even Jimmy's least favoured route through Turkey was in Dry-dock. Seemed strange at the time (We were trying to travel the very direction that so many others were fleeing from). Turning things on its head solved a whole lot of problems. The Sudan visa thing for one. The only route we could find to Egypt at that time was through Israel. Not good if you wanted to visit The Sudan. So in some cases traveling north from South Africa was the way forward.

WooHoo! Our little Serows were in town, Motofreight had done what they said they would and yip, someone came in to the warehouse on the Christmas Holidays to open up for us. Top Shout!

9

A quick check of the essentials, tyre pressures, battery re-connected and electrics all given the once over. Literally within half an hour we were rolling back towards the centre of town and the hostel of choice. Not the best choice but it's coming on towards New Year 's Eve. and the town is filling up with party people. It will serve our needs for now.

I did need time to degrease and check the bikes over properly. I just didn't know what the conditions would be like in the ships hold so they had been sprayed down with a thick sticky grease to protect them. After all they had a few weeks at sea and all that would bring. Soggy wet ships container drizzled in salty sea water? Mmm...

I wasn't sure they'd survive what we had in store for them. They weren't new, in fact they were old technology. Two Yamaha XT225 Serows. A twenty five year old Japanese thumper and a little Brazilian version of only thirteen. Perhaps not the weapon of choice for a lot of motorcycle travellers but it was ours. This was the Trick-cyclist first bike and she knew nothing else. I on the other hand have had a varied bike past. Back when we first met I was travelling on a Triumph. Yip, bigger and more able to carry all your gear and more, but not as agile? I remembered all those times struggling in the sand and not being able to cope. Hell, I remembered the thing trying to kill me! I said the BMW was oversized, to be honest they are all oversized. The whole adventure market has it wrong...Would the little Serow fit the bill? We'll find out.

Time for that run around town and grab all our necessities. Rations for the road. Noodles, vegetables, bread, tuna, tea and coffee. Not everything but enough to get by. Gas canisters, methylated spirit, maps and a pile of odds and sods we thought we'd need. Probably won't need it all but it's something we can adjust along the way and the availability of what we see as necessities. The bikes are gonna be heavy enough and I guess there's gonna be some re-arranging and re-distribution of kit. Jack Sparrow under a bit of pressure here...

By chance friends of the Crazy-one were in town. Rachel and Patrick from the states were in Cape Town at the end of a 6 month cycle ride from Nairobi. They had ridden through Africa 20 years before. It was awesome to sit and chat about what lay before us. But more interesting was how things had changed. Hey at grass roots level African people are still dirt poor, but they've nearly all got a mobile phone. Maybe not the up to date smart phone but they Talk, Text, Internet, WhatsApp, even Bank from them. How can you send money from a wooden shack at the side of a dirt road? Progress even if the mobile phone companies have them by the balls.

Great company and I'm sure I'll enjoy following their journey as they're off on a flight to India the following day. Just great to see them out doing what they love.

We even had time to take a yomp up Table Mountain. Not the best day on the hill. On any hill! Breathing oot my arse if I'm honest.

Time spent on the bike in the summer had taken the last of my fitness and mums home cooking the weeks before we left had seen us both put on a few pounds. The Happy snaps up top a reminder of that. Chubby white tourists. But we survived to enjoy the view over the bay…

The hostel was turning into party town and not in a good way. Can't say we we're enjoying our stay but you can always leave. So we did.

We had chosen to miss last night's new year's party. Ok maybe too exhausted after the days efforts of climbing Table Mountain to be bothered. But lying in our tent, we barely turned over when the midnight fireworks took to the skies. How Rock & Roll are we? Not very it turns out!

Out of town and not soon enough. Up the coast towards The Cederberg and our first real taste of African roads. What an eye opener!

Just a normal road with what looks like a couple of metres of hard shoulder. Normal enough but there's no pavement or cycle path, so every other road user is using that yard of space so to speak.

I lost count of how many cars, bakkies and trucks passed me making some sort of gesture that I should be riding in there to. Bugga

That! Pedestrians, cyclists and everything else is in there. Am I just meant to ignore them? Not to mention every kind of road debris known to man. Broken-down burnt out cars, road rubble and endless piles of rubbish.

Not picking up any nails and the likes this early in the day.

Needless to say they would run me close, but what am I meant to do? Up front as always I could see the Trick-cyclist in any mirrors pulling over the white line as we were bullied by the local drivers. She always questioned it, but I'll be defending my road position me thinks.

We've had this conversation before, more than a few times if be told. Yip, I'm a bit pig-headed sometimes but I was taught to defend my road position and not be bullied by them who'll run you off the road if you let them. You're inviting it on yourself kinda thing. I can even remember those words from my driving instructor when I was learning to drive a car. I'm sure as a cyclist in a foreign land you might think different. Now I'm riding my motorbike, and I know we all deserve to be treated equally.

Rightly or wrongly that's me! I just see it as a lack of respect for your fellow man. Maybe that's just Africa! We'll see!

It wasn't everyone, and being New Year's Day I'm sure it was quieter than normal, so we would survived.

North to Clan William was the direction of choice and then take the 4x4 route into the Cederberg proper. Great road and a great ride compared to the efforts of the road raged locals from the days before. A dusty affair and the first real off-roading. Even had time for a swim in the waterfall plunge pool with the local kids. Well cool. Not quite what I thought I'd be doing, nor them I suppose. I'm sure they were the ones that were more surprised. Pasty Scotsman and a blonde white lady in their swimming pool. But if this is African kids then things will be OK.

We enjoyed the kid's friendship for that's exactly what they were. Good kids but we pushed on feeling better for the cool splash in the pool.

[Video No. 1: **Cederberg**]

The Cederberg was a dry rocky arid place. Yeah, there was bush and scrub along the road but little in the way of the leafy foliage stuff. Strange to see the river running through it to be honest. A green strip of bush either side of the river was the giveaway of its path. In fact if it wasn't for the irrigation systems I'm sure there would be no crops here. Hardly crops but grapes. The Cederberg is into wine. Fine by us. We'll try anything once. Good stuff!

The Maltese Cross

As hiking trails go, it wasn't that hard but the 46 degree temperature nearly saw me off. It had been -9 degrees C when I'd left Edinburgh a few weeks earlier and this really was like hell.

Sunstroke, Heatstroke who knows but I was wobbling on me feet. Lead by the nose and was so glad that there was someone looking after me.

Didn't like this feeling that's for sure.

A bucket full of water and rest in the shade listening to the Work Harder Bird. Some sort of dove but it's exactly what their call sounds like. Just not sure I could work any harder today. A Scotsman in Africa it's just not natural. A pasty Scotsmen anywhere where there's insane heat and sunshine isn't normal. Just not known for being a nation of sun worshipers me thinks.

After dinner that I couldn't really face but knew I did have to eat, an evening of being encouraged to keep on drinking. No none of the wine that's made around here but water just more water. What is it they say? "Hydrate or Die!" Wish I had my Camelback with me now…

Hydrate or Die

Tubes, IV venflow, needles, Saline solution and a willing volunteer. Back in the Marines we would carry all in case of the unforeseen. You can't be caught short wanting and you can't be caught not knowing how to use them.

We would practice stabbing those needles into an orange and on that rare occasion each other. In the jungles of Borneo or deserts of the Middle East, there really is no room for error. Those lectures and training all so vivid now… As far back as the First World War the importance of body fluid replacement was known. While the development of the modern day Intravenous Drip wasn't quite what it is now the military came up with a solution. Rectal Rehydration..

Just as it sounds I'm afraid. Up the bum…

Beggars belief watching a "volunteer" being encouraged to insert a length of plastic tubing where it needs to go. There must have been a hundred others watching while the medic explained what was happening. Fluids being absorbed into the colon. Detailed recording of how much is being absorbed, even the variations of solutions that can be used. A cocktail of salts and rehydration solutions that are available. Just maybe not the Black current sachet you get in the supermarket. Hell, it didn't even have to be fit for consumption. In fact perfect for those areas of the world where the water just not the best of quality. To this day I can't remember exactly how much of the tube had to be inserted but with some silicone based lubricant it was… Yeah, whoops of laughter and gearing from the crowd that was assembled. All bravado and black humour but I'm sure none of us really wanted to be in that position… Not even for the controlled demonstration.

Weeks later out in the Oolu we're put under pressure on exercise. We're all feeling it and some more than others. The Scotsman in me can't drink enough water. It didn't seem possible to drink as much as I was and still have orange coloured pee.

One of the other troops came through our position in a hurry. Shouting and calling out. Just not the norm but one of my mates from Glasgow, Kenny, was going down to dehydration. He's being dragged along behind before collapsing to the ground.

Get out the drip! Where's the saline? Needle, but there's no chance of hitting a vain, it's just not happening. Stick the tube up his arse is the call! It was like a shot of adrenaline, as suddenly he's wide eyed. Bulging out his skull to be honest. Pushing and pulling to gets too his feet to the cries of "I'll bloody well walk out of here." Amazing what will keep you going!... What a thought...

Well and truly I must have been back in the jungle struggling with the heat and fighting dehydration once more. Kicking out and shouting in my sleep. Sometimes the demons come get you but sometimes your dreams are just all too real.

Now I don't know if it's your body's condition that effects your dream state. But that night I stepped back in time into one of those larger than life dreams. Bugga! I was sure it just happened. Maybe something to do with my dehydrated state, salt levels or electrolyte imbalance but it did wake me from my slumber.

Chuckled to myself as I realise where I really was. I'll stick to drinking the water and won't be telling the Crazy-one that story...

Wolfsburg Cracks

A nights rest, albeit my mind a racing and I was on me feet again. Think my partner in crime was checking me out asking herself all sorts of questions. Probably asking what really was going on in my dreams. Not quite sure how I'm gonna handle the heat. I'm pretty sure she was asking herself the same.

Hey maybe unfit and a bit on the chubby side but it was definitely the Scotsman in me that was suffering with the heat. Might just take a few weeks to get used to it. Just hope it don't get any hotter...

The Cracks were in the shade like a semi underground adventure climbing centre, and in the shade All day. What a blessing. Really don't think I could have handled another day in the oven like the day before.

Fab place. We spent hours fallowing the cracks in the cliffs, in and out of sight but as it turns inward there is a different kind of crack in front of us. A labyrinth of rock-way routes and vague pathways to follow. There was nothing straight forward. Up, doon and rooned aboot. Jumping from rock to rock. We stopped many a time to discuss the possibilities (Discuss? Question some of our logic more like). We got it all wrong a few times. Just reset and start again. The description given with the hiking map and permit guide wasn't that accurate, hey it probably added to the day. But when your face down crawling through a tunnel like space and have to turn on to your back to wriggle like a wriggly thing to allow you to make the final twist of the tunnel. You got to ask yourself. Are you doing it right? A challenge no matter how fit you are. A well cool day.

Another chance of a swim in the local pool so why not. A mix of local kids and pasty white tourists like me. Ok! maybe not all like me! But others from the campsites up and down the valley.

A wondrous place, one which is said to have been home to many of the ancient San Bushmen of old. A trip to the local Stadsaal Cave dwellings would set our imaginations alight. Having never experienced cave painting before this was special. They're still here after all this time. Awesome in a big way. Not quite of Banksy standard, not all in great condition but you can almost take yourself back to when the bushman painted them. It's hard to believe that the elephants roamed so freely here back then.

[Video No. 2: **Wolfberg Cracks**]

Some great trails, caves with awesome local artists, a bloody good intro to South Africa. But back to Cape Town to check on the visa extension situation.

90 Days

We were on the assumption that we could travel across South Africa's borders with no real consequence. Visit neighbouring countries like Botswana, Namibia and then returning for the rest of our 90 days.

How wrong were we, the Crazy-one had been here before, I thought she knew best. To be fair she normally did, but the 90 day visa starts and keeps counting no matter if you cross the border in to another country or not. You just can't stop the clock! We had hoped to go to Madagascar amongst others for a few months or more. Returning to South Africa to collect our bikes and carry on. The 90 day thing would make it difficult. But this is Africa I suppose. It's never straight forward and I'm starting to realize it.

The cost, and the possibility of change, the hanging around waiting on a decision was enough for us to change our plans and escape town. Madagascar would have to wait for another day. It was something we had dreamed of for some time, but it's always good to have something on the back burner I suppose… for now that's where it'll have to stay.

A trip around the Cape Peninsula was on the cards. Just because it's there. You just can't not go! The ride by Table Mountain and head south was a bit windy, but worth it. Stand in line with the rest of the tourists to get your picture taken at the cape. But the real entertainment was in the car park though, hilarious. I'm sitting eating me sandwich watching the baboons terrorize the tourist. Happy Days. It wasn't my stuff they were stealing. Nasty I know but made me giggle.

2

Southern comforts

Bulgarian Starter Clutch!

You don't need bike trouble at any time but Wow, I thought we had left this back in Bulgaria. The bolts fixing the starter clutch to the back of the rotor had sheared and stuck in the starter clutch gear effectively seizing the engine on Shaun our Japanese bike. Yip, it's a sheep thing! We spent nearly 3 weeks stripping down the engine back in the summer. We did learn so much in doing so. With YouTube, Haynes Manual and a few Facebook friends we could rebuild it. We made the most of the time hanging around waiting on parts sightseeing and looking at houses. We loved the place, could see ourselves living there. Just didn't faze us…

That was then and this is now. I just can't believe its came back to haunt us here in South Africa

After speaking to the auto electrician back home it might have been the poor starting that had the effect of loosening the bolts. Maybe!

As much as we were enjoying South Africa there was no need of house hunting. Have tent, Will Travel but the bolts had sheared again. No other damage so we got the local scooter guys to help us pull out the rotor the starter clutch and the starter clutch gear. Put the engine case back together and gave it a kick start.

WooHoo! All Is good. A 25 year old bike in Africa. There's one good reason…

It'll take time to arrange but we could try get the new starter clutch down the road somewhere. Not sure I would have gotten any local help if I'd been riding a more modern high tech bike.

Cape Agulius. The most southerly tip of Africa and where the Indian and Atlantic oceans meet. You just got to go. At least to say you've been but hey, it was kinda cool too. Met some nice people as we ate lunch at the side of the road. An invite to their home for something cool. South African hospitality. Great start to the journey north. I say north but east for the moment as we follow our version of the garden route.

[Video No. 3: **Sunshine & Penguins**]

A couple of days in Swellen Dam with good Wi-Fi helped us sort out some parts further east in Port Elizabeth. So we kinda have a target for now. But plenty of things in between to be going on with. DeHell and The Karoo, rougher roads than the normal Garden Route but who says we had to stick to the tourist route.

Gravel Travel that's us. Well as long as we can stay on the bike. The 1st off for the Trick-cyclist. A long day in the saddle to be honest and just a lapse of concentration. She was ok just some light bruising and a few scuffs for Shaun. Picked herself up and got on with it…

Route 62 – Ronnie's Sex Shop probably a must for most who travel this route and to be fair there wasn't much on this route. But a welcome distraction from the heat of the day.

No not the Knocking Shop you think it would be. Apparently when Ronnie was on holiday one year friends were looking after the place and painted in the SEX bit on the sign. Someone with a sense of humour…

If it brings in the customers let it be. So he did and the people come. Strange collection of bras hanging from the ceiling but I won't ask why. Scared of what the answer will be.

Rolling along through the favoured names of the Garden Route of George, Wilderness and Knysna, for everyone we met along the way had their favourite. All were cool in fact Wilderness we loved, easy days hiking and paddling up the river but not quite us. Remember the gravel thing. After the beauty of Knysna, a truly stunning waterfront town with marina and housing to match. Wealth oozing out of it and we head for the sticks once more.

We're heading for the interior of The BaviannsKloff. An iconic place for enduro riders to test how big their balls are! I'm sure its many more things to more people. But its time to test out Jack & Shaun. Jack as in Sparrow, something that came out of an auto correct spelling thingy whilst texting and Shaun as in a Sheep thing from the Crazy-ones first trip to Scotland. A sheep sticker for her bike, it kinda stuck. Maybe a chance of bit of wildlife too. Can't say we've seen a whole lot of that yet. The Western Cape seems to have used up that natural resource.

Turn off the main road and head for the hills. Yip, the wealth is left behind and you find yourself traveling through the workers accommodation. Logging communities by the looks of things and there is no spare anything here. Another side of South Africa. Maybe not all that comfortable with it yet. Just can't get my head around what's what and who's who. I'm sure they're good people but I am a bit wary. Better when I hit the BaviannsKloff proper.

Wildlife conservation area with a price to travel through but we don't expect to be let into any of the big wildlife parks on our bikes. Just the way of things but if they had any of the big cat, elephants and the likes it would make sense I suppose.

Rock Art and Rock Caves of Makkedaat, we even spent the night in one. Ok, it had been developed into a crazy mix of half cave come half log cabin but a quirky place that we both enjoyed. Our first big bed since leaving home what a treat. Could have got used to that one!

But there was more exploring to be done. Caves and kloofs a plenty, so a day or two off the bike to do exactly that. Felt a bit like one the old Boer Trekkers, how they must have felt while scouring this land many years ago. Amazing, Truly Amazing. Can't beat walking up the riverbed in search of what lives there. From Multi-coloured frogs to tortoise and some you'd rather not meet. Yip, and the Vervet monkeys were in attendance.

Should have taken note of that one as we moved on and back to camping later in the day.

The ever laughing Ha-De-Da Ibis and Baboons are just about all we saw. In fact BaviaannsKloof was Dutch for Valley of The Baboons but this place was more than that. A rugged snapshot of South Africa and yeah, I can understand why Enduro Riders come here to measure up. Awesome trails set up for 4x4 so just up our street to. An all day trip up and over the mountains to meet a Dutchmen. Pancakes at the Sweaty Dutchmen's restaurant in town that is! Great day and riding without your luggage is a pleasure. Always… Just need to remember that we've got a long way to go and have to keep the bikes in one peace. The Trick-cyclist wobbling and finding it tricky or maybe reminding herself of the weeks before in Dehell. It's a confidence thing me thinks, but I have confidence in her. Years of mountain biking will see her through and the confidence will come back I'm sure…

What can I say as we were out exploring the little Vervet fookas were exploring our tent. That probably makes it sound like curiosity. Let's Trash The Tent More Like. Let's just throw stuff around and when I get too excited I'll just smear shit over your tent. Oh! on the inner as well.

Vervet? Kinda cute lookin but…just not. Devilish little buggers.

Picked all our cooking stuff out of the dam, pots, pans, and the stove. Gathered some water and set about washing the tent. Felt like the Ha-De-da's were laughing at me as I removed the vervet DNA…

There's a lesson in here… never trust the Vervet…

The ride through the rest of The Baviaans made up for it though.

Notoriously known for not having the best of trail conditions. Torrents of water flowing from the mountains making it impassably for many months of the year. Numerous streams flowing in to the central river. Most with concrete fords but not all. Not that all the water stayed in the river though. That low lying valley allowing it to reach out beyond the banks of the river. A wet affair indeed!

Aptly named by the Dutch Boer Trekkers as there were Baboons everywhere. Lining the trail as we went. Basking in the sunshine and the heat of the morning but they'd scatter as the bikes came near, running for cover of the bush. The more dominant males standing Sentry till all were safely in the bush before making their escape. A game of hide and seek as they never went far from the road but rather just out of sight.

Wet boots, wet jeans from the Recce of the riverbeds we had to cross and a squelch as we walked. Stopping for lunch we could strip off the wet stuff and ring-out before leaving to dry. Our turn to stand Guard as the baboons were never far away. They'd steel anything given half a chance. Still smiling though, we had thoroughly enjoyed the ride through BaviaannsKloof. Just topped off a great couple of days.

[Video No. 4: **BaviannsKloff**]

Into town from here, a date with Mr Yamaha and a hope that they've got the parts for Shaun.

3

Away with the fairies

Port Elizabeth had everything. Hotels and guesthouses galore but a few nights camping in the garden at the hostel is good enough. Shaun was in safe hands and a chance to take me lady out for slap up pizza. Can't have the ostrich fillets we ate back in Wilderness every night.

Gave me some time to check the bikes over before turning north out of town.

Hogsback

You gotta have somewhere to aim for. It sounded just the job. Hiking along the Amatola Trail and a few days chilling in a town which will throw you back to the sixties and Away With the Fairies. That's maybe why it took so long for them to get back to us about the hiking. They said they could organise the permits and anything else for that matter. In their own time obviously. Weren't sure right up until we got there if we could or would get a permit to hike. Even then we had to wait for the boss to turn up.

[Video No. 5: **HogsBack Riding into Heaven**]

The Permit was all there so we could go hiking straight away. A decent briefing about the trail and what looked like a decent map. The owners wife introduced herself and mentioned something about an incident at one of the mountain huts. Said we should be aware of our surrounding and aware of who's around. Keep your processions close to you kinda thing... Ok we will and No more was said.

Picked up by the 4x4 in the morning and the boss was there to see us off. Closes the door but hangs around sheepishly outside then decides to open the door again. "*It would be remiss of me not to tell you about the incident up at the mountain hut about a month ago*". Hey, we stopped him and mentioned his wife had told us. "*Oh in that case you'll be fine. There's a local guy up near the hut tending his goats and what not, he'll give you a hand to start your fire. It happened one of the few times of the year when he was away visiting family. You'll be fine*"...

Then the girl who was dropping us off just sounded a bit sheepish about the incident. Changed the subject quite quickly if I remember.

Driving through various homesteads and shanty towns it wasn't long before we were out in our own. Six days of just us. WooHoo!.

We enjoyed the hiking even if the trail was a bit overgrown at times. Didn't think I'd be bush whacking quite as much but still good to be out. No one to be seen not even at any of the mountain huts but it was fine by us. That was until day three when we walked into a couple of locals with their homemade looking shotgun. Not that we felt threatened not even bothered by the dozen or so hunting dogs they had with them but it was the conversation that got me thinking. They knew all about the trail and the huts and that we were going to Hogsback. Even knew how many days it would take. In that case they knew when we would be at any given hut.

Mmm... I'm sure they were ok guys but if they knew, then anyone who wanted to make it their business would too.

Onto the hut where the incident took place. Fire already started for us. Well cool. The goat herder off in the distance and no sign of anyone else. Very peaceful. So much so with water in abundance we strung up the water bag and had a shower in the yard.

Naked Time!:-) Hey it put a smile on my face and it felt good to be clean for a while. Great to sleep out on the veranda too. Can't beat being outdoors, at peace in the StaryNight Hotel something we did at almost all the huts.

It all finished with a wet final night, but we even enjoyed that. Shower and washed my walking gear just in time for the Crazy-one to barbecued my socks. She says she didn't mean it but I'm sure she had clean sock envy.

Lying outside on the verandah once more listening to the frog chorus. Bliss but It didn't last as the wind direction changed. Blowing and turning the rain directly into our sheltered spot. Run for the cover of the hut, but better than getting wet eh?. Not the best way to start the trudge back into town. A bit of a disappointment. Wet, grey with any and all beauty hidden in the clouds, but all in all the trail was pretty cool.

Away With the Fairies once more. Beer pizza and chat with some Brit Overlanders. Muck & Malarky, Bill and Jean. Even found out Jenny & Craig that we had met in Cape Town had passed us bye heading for the UK whilst we were hiking? Pity as we'd like to have had the chance to catch up. Hey they had their own plan.

The chance of a Wi-Fi catch up with the world. Yip, curiosity got the better of us. What was the incident at the mountain hut?

Bastards! Keep an eye on your valuables turned out to be armed robbery and gang rape. Yip, that's what I said gang rape. To think we slept outside at that hut. Shit, to think we got naked in the yard and showered there. It also transpired that the day before our permit was issued that a local families event was cancelled due to security fears. Bastards!

I felt angry but the Trick-cyclist felt betrayed. If we had all the facts we could have made our own decisions but that was taken away from us. In fact never given to us. More adventurous than most and can make her own mind up I know. But I wouldn't have put her in danger like that, that's for sure.

4

Running for the hills

We hit the road and out of town, Lesotho is calling us. Great roads and trails but can't stop thinking of what's just happened. The good folk at Away With the Fairies gave me stuff to think about. We've not wild camped as much as we thought we would have. In fact only a couple of times to date. South Africa has been cheap so we've used campsites and hostels most of the way. So when we camped at the side of the road that night I lay awake for hours. The other one sleeps so soundly, but me? Just can't sleep until I'm convinced no one's gonna disturb us during the night.

Determined nothings gonna happen on my watch.

Lesotho. Across the border and we're heading for Malealea Lodge. Amongst other things they do horse riding tours. Not got a wealth of saddle time under my belt but how hard can it be. Six day tour of Lesotho. Taking local trails and staying in local villages. Thinking this might be a great way to meet them too.

Didn't make Malealea but we did meet the locals. Lesotho is well populated and to be honest we struggled to find somewhere to camp so we asked at the local shop. I say local shop but to the untrained eye there was no tell tales signs of that. They were a bit surprised to say the least, in fact just laughed out loud. But off he went to the tool shed and brought back a rake. Raked us a pitch next to the parked up tractor and pointed out the family long drop. The whole family came down from the hill to watch us pitching the tent. Chat and a photo shoot and all was good. Such a friendly family. Easier nights sleep that's for sure!

Off up the track to Malealea in the morning which really was a class act. The lodge maybe showing its age as it's been around for a while but well cool with some great community projects going on. All the ponies were owned by locals and all the guides were local to. They really were trying to give something back in support of the village around them.

My Lesotho pony

The Overlanders we met at Hogsback turned up just in time to photograph the grand depart. Yeah really, must have looked frightening me!. Or just frightened, I'm not sure which. Well out of my depth! Before this I've had the Sum total of 5hrs in the saddle. Not really that confident but hey, no way out of it now.

Off down through the village at an easy pace which was fine but if you know Lesotho the easy trail was about to end.

Wow! Off downhill towards the river. I'm not sure I would have the nerve to ride my bike down here. Pushing back on the pommel of the saddle and digging in with my stirrups, I managed to stay on. Glad to get to the river but then the realisation of where the trail went next.

Up the other side. Bugga I wouldn't have had the talent to ride my bike up it. But the Little Lesotho Pony? Nothing fazed it! Even when he lost his footing he just stopped. Steady himself. Pulled his legs in and carried on. Just awesome.

Jessie the yodeling cowgirl meanwhile? Ok not yodeling just laughing out loud at my impression of a cowboy. Well nothing fazed her. She had been brought up with horses. She taught me enough to stay in the saddle and enjoy the ride. Six full riding days, just Incredible!

We were heading for Semonkong, a lodge some three days ride away. Easy days on the trail and I genuinely believe it's a wonderful way to travel, it's an easy pace. You never really have to watch your feet, you rarely have to look out for other traffic. In my case all I had to do was hang on... hairy times when I really did say WTF closed my eyes and hung on. Yeah more than once that's for sure. But what a ride!

I think originally Jessie had thought of buying a horse for riding across Lesotho. Even she admits it would have been hard. So over populated, so over grazed. The competition for such grazing would have brought us into conflict with the local villagers. Me thinks we would have struggled a bit, so this was about the right compromise. Maybe something we can put on the back burner for now. Yeah more for the back burner!

Back to camp and a treat of a real room. Jessie's birthday and she's worth it! As long as there's no Yodeling...

[Video No. 6: **My Lesotho Pony**]

Black Pass

Southern Africa has the highest concentration of lightning strikes anywhere in the world apparently. Only Small areas of Venezuela and the DRC having more. The highlands of Lesotho, well they're at the heart of it. The bikes all packed, just payed up our bill and checking the map for the day. Put in the route on the satnav the best we could, then... Crack!

Flash Bang, and I'm convinced my bike has taken a lightning strike. Nearly jumped out my skin if I'm honest. Even the woman in the community Shop came running out. She had seen what happened and could see the look on my face. I've no idea what she said to me. Everything's a blur. Wow!

The sky had been looking a bit dark and cloudy but there was nothing to suggest me the strike was imminent. Bugga what a let off it seems. The bike was right between us... It certainly rattled me.

Well we were ready to go, so let's go. We're following the old road which zigzagged across southern Lesotho. No one at camp knew how much was tarmac and what was not. Chinese work fast around here but we would find out.

A mixed bag from Malealea to Semonkong. A full day's riding, a journey which had taken three days on the Pony riding the direct route. But we settled back into being back on the bikes. Resupplied from the local store and we're off proper.

How far had the Chinese tarred the hillside? Well pretty far, as we biked up the new road. A shiny new ribbon of the black stuff. Which was fine to be honest if not a touch surreal. Brand new road with no traffic and the Chinese, well they just took the direct route wherever they could. Never been down in first gear on the road before. Ever!

Reminded me of The Rannoch Moor back home in Scotland with weather to match.

Down the other side and we meander our way from and through every village in the valley which mattered. Lines of mud being purposely placed across the road. Intrigued for an age, what was it all about? Ok maybe not every village but enough of them to make you think.

It seemed this was pieces of the termite mound placed out on the road in the hope of being crushed by the passing traffic. The powdered remnants then swept up and mixed into the dung type plaster-mix for the walls of their Rondavaal Round-Houses. Ingenious No?

We did turn off the shiny new road heading for Sehlabatebe National Park come Wilderness Area. Not that we made it. Long into the day and we were just happy to find a spot for ourselves to camp. We had been hand-railing the border for a while which basically follows the natural cliff edge of the high ground. Great chance to sit and enjoy what we could of the view in front of us. Birds of Prey surfing the thermals, surging up from the cliffs in front of us.

Didn't last long I'm afraid. The rains came quick. Quickly followed by the rumble of thunder. Yip, you guessed it. What came next? Flash, Bang and flashes of lightning. I'd never seen it so intense and last so long it seemed like half the night. The wind snarled and blew around the tent forcing us to hang on to it many a time. You got to start wondering when is it coming. When's it our turn? The lightning thing had struck a real fear in us. But we convinced ourselves that the bikes were the highest point and any strike would hit them first.

Light it Up

There's many variations on information of how to survive a lightning strike.

Avoid tall trees, Lightning tends to strike them 1st. Check, there is none.

If caught out in the open, head for the valley or lower ground. Eh, Check, a hole in the ground is all there was.

Remember the 30/30 rule. If after seeing lightning, and you can't count to thirty before hearing thunder, head indoors. Thirty? It's like being at the longest firework display every. There is no indoors!

Make your way to a substantial building with plumbing electrify etc. Sheds and bus shelter don't offer any real protection, Mmm… don't know what they would say about the tent. Not a good Idea me thinks…

It's safer to be in a vehicle if your outdoors. What? I just don't think the bike was ever thought about.

Mmm… I could go on and on, but we just had no other options open to us. Jesse not yodeling now but she sits up to sort out the roof of the tent which was leaking. Just jammed a towel up there really but I did encourage her to lie back down suggesting she was now the highest thing around and I'm not sure about the metal poles of the tent and how it might attract any strike.

Those extra guy ropes we left back in Blighty might have helped our now sadly leaking and misshapen tent. But hey it's just got to last out the night. Right?

Not exactly sun splitting the trees in the morning but it was calm enough to pack up and crack on. Ok bad choice of words. Thankfully with our tent and us are still intact. Not the best campsite we've ever had. Not exactly our best choice but you live and learn. Might just remember that one…

What followed was one of the wettest days in a long while On through the edges of the park and back up over the Black Pass. More river crossings than I can remember. Not all of them that deep but deep enough, masses of water flowing off the side of the mountain. Forgot how many times I got off the bike to wade through those torrents of water. Scouting out the best route for the bikes. Endless it seemed. But it did bring a smile to our faces. We made the best of it and paddled on!

[Video No. 7: **Blackpass**]

We eventually got back to some sort of track come – road, even found a lodge. Well somewhere to stay. Shower and a beer always go down well. We deserved it!

5

The Sani-Pass

Back to School

We were heading for a 4x4 route over the mountains to Mahoklong.
Back in Malealea the good folk there gave us the idea. Up and over
the top, it sounded worth a look at the time.

What a trail. Rough as they come but cool too. Not the tourist
route for sure. We spent most of the day winding onward and upward.
Struggling at times with the rocky trail and with the bikes fully loaded
it was a real struggle but then the inevitable happened.

Jimmy dropped his bike!

Now I've lost count of the Trick-cyclists thrills and spills and how
she accounts for drops, spills or even the bike falling over on its own
but this was my first off since Mongolia some two or more years
before. Glad it brought such glee to her face. Yip, she couldn't hide it.
Written all over her face. Jimmy was human... hey, no real damage
but for some reason the clutch wouldn't work. We had dozens of kids
around us and we were just laughing it off. Happy snaps all around.
What we gonna do?.

One off the kids took us to see the school teacher. You can stay the
night. Cool. A night in the teacher's staff room. A new one on me but
we pitched to tent inner anyway, thought that would be enough until
the night watchmen arrives and just sat in the chair in the corner.
Mmm... Tent outer on and eventually we got to sleep. Never felt
threatened by this strange situation but just bizarre!

The rains had come back to haunt us in the night. As we lay there focussed by those tent illuminating lightning flashes closely followed by those rumbles of thunder. The soaked track and a dodgy clutch played heavily on my mind for what was to come. For what was to be possible for the morrow?

As we waited for the rain to stop we decided to go back down the trail. So close to the other side but we would struggle with the soaked trail on the downhill never mind the up. The right choice in the end.

Good memories from our night in the school house. Great kids too!

The weather blanket had lifted and we wiggled our way from track to trail to roadside and things were looking brighter, we were making progress. Busy road junction with loads of traders and people hanging around the local store. Buses left and right. To busy looking around when I ran over something. As I checked in my mirrors I could see Heidi checking something out on the road. I waited and as she caught up. There's a group of locals hanging around the junction, they started shouting and swearing. Shit I'd ran over a puppy. Not sure who's it was or even if it was dead or not. I just knew I wasn't hanging around. Let's just go.

Yip I felt guilty. I love dogs I've had dogs but I'm not getting myself lynched for that one. There's no pets in Africa and there certainly not cared for. If it had been, it wouldn't have been in the road. Survival of the fittest and If they survive then there might be a use for then. Shepherd dogs or guard dog I suppose.

I'm sure the animal lover didn't approve, but my mind was made up. Let's go and she went along with it but her face said she wasn't happy. Hey! I was an animal lover to. I was racked with guilt for days and she reminded me of it at every opportunity. Still don't like talking about it. Guilt, shame and sorrow all rolled into one. Not a good feeling, and yeah I've got some....

Keep on rolling and we did enjoy the journey even though it was a bit tainted by the puppy incident.

White lodge before Mahoklong a peaceful place to stay before town. More tourist for a change. The usual chat of where you've been and where your going, what not. Oh you need to speak to Richard our son he's been everywhere. I remember this. Trying to press all your knowledge on someone before you know what they've already done themselves. They never once asked what we had done before. Sounds familiar and it did bring a smile to my face. Heidis to as I caught her glancing look in my direction. She has had it all before. You don't write two travel books without those moments I suppose.

Mahoklong for a resupply before the SaniPass. Not that we needed that much but we had the idea of dropping off some supplies at the hostel on top. This for the hiking we wanted to do later along the length of the Drakensburg.

Yet another shiny new road to the top. Pleasure to ride after the disastrous 4x4 trail.

The Sani Top BackPacker were cool with us staying and dropping off those supplies. Named and dated for pick up later.

Fab dinner and a beer. We deserve it! Not much to see on top as the mountain side is clagged in. But we spent our time reading the messages on the wall of the highest pub in Southern Africa apparently. Kept us amused for a bit before another night in our tent.

[Video No. 8: **The SaniPass before The Top Gear Digger**]

Wow glad we were going down the pass as there was so many broken down BMWs trying to make their way up. Ok maybe they were just taking their happy snaps. It was just a thought…

The trail was as rough as they come. In fact we had been told that the upper section had been completely washed away during the recent heavy rains. We managed as we changed direction through the many switch back sections whilst riding through the clagg. It didn't seem that bad but out of the cloud appeared not one but two diggers. Repairing the upper section of the road. Banked high were rock filled cages (Gabion Baskets) which were to support their efforts of the new road. The operator momentarily stopping to lift the bucket high to allow us through. If truth be told it only added to the day.

Khotso

Underburg was on the horizon, ok down below and across the border into South Africa. What a beautiful run into town. What a beautiful town to be honest. Great place to stay in Khotso Farm horse-trails and backpackers. Good feeling straight away. Pitched our tent next to Phill & Angies truck before escaping to town. There's a Yamaha shop for Shaun. He needs more attention, rear shock this time. God only knows how the Trick-cyclist can cope with it. The shock needs re-gassed and serviced. The Gravel Travel thing taking its toll on him.

We're knackered, Shaun's gonna take longer than we thought and we're running out of time if we want to see any of the battlefields never mind all our other plans. The big trek along the Drakensburg might need a rethink. In fact it does. We have a rest instead. A few days with easy hiking building ourselves up, just generally enjoying Underburg and the Khotso Farm. A bit of paddling down the river to which was an absolute hoot!:-).

[Video No. 9: **Just Paddling**]

Steve Black the owner came out with one of the best lines I ever heard. He's an ultra-marathon runner with a difference. Got to chatting, talking about my one and only marathon, my ongoing injuries and training wows. He told me of his double marathon schedule. My chin dropped.

Double? Apparently "80km a day isn't comfortable but it's manage-able." As he tells me of his race across South Africa. Incredible guy. How can you keep up a double marathon schedule day after day…

Spent my time whittling a set of nunchucks, well Jesse when she not riding horses wanted to learn a bit of Karate, so we did. Made a punch pad out of a foam roll mat, Bo staff out of fence rail and a set of nunchucks out of the walking pole I had carried from the Amatola trail. African Knob-Wood. Can't just throw it away. Learned a little traditional nunchucks in the past and always wanted to dedicate more time to them. Now's my chance and the Crazy-one was keen to learn. Just good to be training again to be honest.

We did start up in Lesotho whilst on the Pony trek. I was determined to get my training going again. Heidi had asked what I was doing and can I show her some stuff. Well it turned into basic punching kicking and simple throws. Before I knew it I had a Dojo of 2 as our guide wanted to learn to.

Well rested at Khotso we decide on a shorter hike back up the SaniPass and a few days along the southern end of the Drakensburg. A much shorter hike that's for sure but we enjoyed what we did. We got a good feel for the place. Met some of the local goat herders. Local boys taking their journey into manhood. They spend six months or so up here tending the goats. Couldn't think of anything less appealing. Walking around with my blanket on tending goats. Just not a cool look. Most did come over and chat, just wish they didn't bring their dogs but I did have me nunchucks in hand when they got to close. Never needed to use them in anger but it made me feel safer. Made me feel safer on a night time to. Don't mind saying after the Amatola incident the nunchucks were never far from hand on a night time. I feel safer and I couldn't live with myself if anything happened on my watch. I know Heidi would say she doesn't need protecting for I know she's an accomplished traveller. Street smarts don't always save you...

I see the way African blokes are with her, with any female really. They'd be chatting her up in front of me. I don't think blanket boy in his under pants and gummy boots had a chance of a date but it didn't stop them trying. It even became easier to say we were married.

Needless to say I slept less most nights we slept out.

Great times in Underberg even found the Best Cream Tea in Africa. Pucketty Farm, could have stayed for that alone but all good things, and all that!. We have to push on if we want to see the battlefields. We had been reading up on the Boers and the Zulus for that matter and didn't want to miss them.

6
Kwa Jim's

Time for a few days in Kwa Zulu Natal and a bit of hiking, hey! no time to see all of the Drakensburg but a final look before we move on. Glorious to be honest. But on we must go.

The Battlefields heading for Dundee and Ladysmith all great stops even if the rain followed us.

All forgotten when we reached Isandlwana though. The site of one of the most disastrous defeats for the British army. We all can remember the story of Rourke's Drift and the Zulu wars but Isandlwana is what came before and I don't think I've ever visited such a moving site. The Colours (The Union Jack) fluttering in the breeze makes the hairs on the back of your neck stand on end. Shivering tales of death and many piles of white-washed stones in front of me. From my high vantage point I could relive the battle from there. Eerie if I'm honest.

Old Marine me, and it's hard to come to terms with the incompetence at such a high level in the army. But without going into it all, that's exactly what it was. Can't believe we follow these bastards into battle, but we take the kings shilling and do our duty. All of these things race around inside my head. Probably gonna stay there and only come to the surface at times like this. Vanquish the demons another day…

Rourke's Drift is only around the corner so to speak but we need time to process this.

We go the next day and re-live what we can remember. A story of the brave. Heavily outnumbered the small company of men that stood

41

between the Zulu masses and the ruling classes of the empire. What a thought. An incredible story was told.

I'm not one to cast doubt over any man's bravery. Was it glorified to hide the dishonour of defeat the days before? Who knows! I for one hold these men in high regard but feel shameful when I think of those who lead them there, as it was undoubtedly for their benefit.

God Bless the Fallen.

When I read about the after-math and that the wounded attackers were bayoneted where they lay, my mind went into overdrive of what they all went through. Changed days when you hear the story of Sgt Al Blackman RM putting an Afghan insurgent out of his misery on the battlefield and then being imprisoned for it.

There were 11 Victoria Crosses award after Rourke's Drift.

I'm not immune to the loss of life on both side and I was just as moved at the memorial for the Zulu Warriors that fell that day.

It didn't matter where we went in South Africa we were always reminded of what had went before. I'm sure there will be more as we travel the length of this continent.

Move on with a sorrow in my heart. Something that was to remain with me for most of the trip.

[Video No. 10: **Giraffes**]

A short excursion in to Swaziland for it was short and wet. Could do with less of the cloud thing but the local farmers need the rain and who I'm I to deny them. North in the direction of the border. The South African / Botswanan border that is. We've got time but why hang around when it's as wet as it was.

Nelspruit, Hodspruit, Polokwane and more all just names on the map to me really but we push on.

We did visit a local endangered species sanctuary one afternoon. Great in itself but as we re-supplied in town there were people at the car parked next to us. Ah UK plates! Never got much more of the explanation out when one of them blurts out. "I know you" pointing to the travel writer who had forgotten. Really! Turns out Bob had bought one of Trick-cyclist travel books at a HuBB UK meet. Small world eh…

Well the conversation turned into we need a campsite. Ok follow us we'll show you the way. That turned into five nights sleeping on Mel & Andys sofa bed. What a place. Beautiful cottage on the dam. Turns out Andy's a Master Leathersmith and they all run a small leather company come shop in the compound next door. Awesome! New friends, great company and a chance to service the bikes. Rest and a Wi Fi catch up.

Turns out I have some skills and truly loved working in the workshop with Andy.

He even offered me an apprenticeship. I'll be giving that one some thought that's for sure… It's a Leather Thing.

We would spend the evening talking of travels and the adventures we'd all had. Talked about South African drivers and being bullied on the roads. Everyone laughs and Heidi say she just can't wait to see me ride through a big African city. Kinshasa or Kampala and the likes. As if everything has been all tame till then.

Everyone asking what's the plan, the route and how we're going to get back to Europe. A suggestion of the ferry to Turkey. Mmm… not if I can help it. Italy or Greece would be good enough for me.

Chit-Chat about how we met which always raises an eyebrow. Love telling people that we met in Mongolia. We chat about the bikes and how small they were in comparison to most who travel overland. Bob even had one of the oversized BMW GS's. Mmm… there's a bike out there for everyone and every journey I say. Maybe not often enough but I do tell them the story of how the GS guys helping me out when I was in Mongolia having a hard time. When I poke fun at GS riders it's only that. A bit of fun. Good Times.

7
Day 101

We've had a few ups and downs over the last months but always came through it I thought. But there's frosty times crossing Botswanan and I'm not sure Heidi really wanted to be with me or just be with me to travel through Africa. I'm not here for that. I just want to travel with her and wherever that took us... true Jimmy style, that doesn't come over very good and sounds like some sort of ultimatum. Not what I wanted to say. Love this girl and wish I could make her understand.

I should really learn to speak. What an idiot...

90 days in South Africa and it wasn't all-out scary driving but it did have its moments. Main roads best avoided we thought. Gravel Travel! It's the way forward.

It's what we like, little roads and gravel trails and South Africa had enough of them. The Cederberg, The Karoo, The Baviaanskloof then crossing Lesotho most of it off the beaten track and truly wonderful.

Every time we'd travel a main road we'd see the type of nuggets we'd been trying to avoid. Up close and personal. Hey maybe they were trying to check my SatNav as they went by. Trucks, Backkies, Minibus taxis even The Presidential Cavalcade, they all wanted to be close to you. Never expected to be taken out of the game by some smartly dressed bloke in Beamer.

Downtown Windhoek Yamaha Namibia.

I had been monitoring an oil leak for some time. Over a year in fact. But it wasn't bad. Well that was until crossing Botswana. Not another bike to be seen in the country never mind a bike shop. Not quite true but a BMW at the border 2 coppers and some sort of Hells Angel. Strange really. Leather vested individual who seemed well out of place.

Anyway had to top up the bike engine with car engine oil. Big mistake as it just leaked more. Really wished then that I had paid attention to what the engine could cope with. Basic engine oil, not the stuff with performance enhancing additives. God only knows what was going on now.

Needed a cunning plan, not really! just kept topping it up after every hour of riding. Let it cool down and moved on. Eventually we crossed into Namibia and into Windhoek. The land of plenty bike shops and a Yamaha Valhalla.

Dropped off Jack Sparrow for a second time for them to work on his oil leak. Twos up and into town. That's when The Beamer attacked. When you've got your guard down.

He brushes up the side of me at the junction (Obviously to get a better look at my SatNav). He continues out into the carriage way running over my foot and squeezing me between him and my bike. Didn't squeal much. Piggy Impersonator if I'm honest…

At least he done the Christian Thing! No pun intended but he helped me off the roadside and took me to the Roman Catholic Hospital.

Pain killing injection and an X-ray. That'll be 1500 bucks please and here's your prescription. Mmm… need some pain relief to swallow that one? Sacky The Beamer Driver (strange that Big flash car, you'd think it come with its own SatNav) did follow up with a few phone calls and an offer of "if there is anything I can do…"

The sitting around bump started me into writing my journal again. Something that I'd neglected since traveling with the Trick-Cyclist. Time sitting in the campsite to reflect on a few things.

No broken bones, just a minuscule chip (which wasn't visible on the X-ray to me really) and a big bit of swelling. Not much to look at, but bugga it hurt and I couldn't weight bare on it. Foot up and let nurse Heidi take care of me. That honeymoon didn't last long though. She's not the sympathetic type. Didn't need much sympathy really just a hand here and there. More strained faces and tantrums…

Hey we're still working each other out! I think that's gonna take longer than I thought.

Life been a touch strained lately. We've been in each other's pockets for longer than 101 days. Some 10 month since we both quit work and hit the road. Hardly been apart in all that time. More than just in each other's pockets. Not many secrets between us so in each other's phones and all that entales. Couldn't help reading a messenger message from of her old travel buddies, Nigel. Made me think she just seen me as a part of the journey, just handy to have around and not a part of her life…

Strained yeah but as we talked about the possibility of my foot not healing I'm sure I could see through the look on her face. She'd go on to Angola without me…

Probably most of it was me. Maybe a bit road weary, but kinda wish I hadn't seen her messenger thingy. Maybe I'm just tired of people asking "so how do you 2 know each other?" Brother and sister? Cousins? Oh! Are you a couple? That one hurts. Only me it seems. From the ordinary Joe in the street to the nosey border guards.

There is a few years between us but it doesn't seem to bother her or so she says. Me feeling my age and a touch insecure. Starts me thinking. Mmm… Not always good at saying the right things, but I think we all need lessons in that one. Or is it a male thing?

As long as I'm honest I'm sure we'll work it out… Work harder! Work harder!

Boots and All

The conclusion of all our plans was wait and see, wait and see when or if I can get a boot on my foot. But when the day came to re-visit the Angolan Embassy I was still hobbling around on my crutches.

WooHoo! They'd given us a month. Oh the realisation of what that meant. Best try my boots on. No joy but we stripped out Heidis hiking boot and managed to get it on over the strapping on my foot. Not the best solution but it's on and we could make do. Just need to see if I can ride the bike.

Wow! The pain of trying to change gear was incredible. I could down-shift by kicking down with my heel but trying to up-shift just wasn't gonna happen anytime soon.

Broke out some of the fencing wire from the spares bag and wrapped it around the gearshift. Adding a peace of para-cord from down there by my left foot I ran it up and over the fuel tank, securing the lose end to the right-hand side of the handle bars. Left it loose so not to hinder the steering and the wire end prevented the para-cord frying from the heat of the engine. Modern-day Suicide Shifter!

Test ride around town with my crutches strapped to the side of the bike and the jobs a badger... I did struggle to get off the bike so the Trick-cyclist had to be on hand with the crutches. It did take a bit of getting used to with the clutch being on the left and throttle on the right. A bit of freewheeling was required, as I took my hand off the throttle to reach across to tug on the suicide shifter. You just had to check your mirrors and look for that gap in the traffic behind.

If there was ever one single day that could have change our journey it was that one. A tipping point for sure. Visa in hand Heidi would have gone to Angola without me and I'm sure I would have shipped my bike home from there. After our recent ups and downs I'm sure it would have been the end of us. That's if there really was gonna be an us!

8

Desert Days

The Zebra Pans

There was no way I was gonna manage the hike that everyone takes out to the Giant Sand Dunes at Sossusvlei, but a similar route to Solitaire and on to the Zebra Pans could well be possible. A good test for what lay ahead further up the Skeleton Coast and Kaokoland.

Managed to blag a tourist permit for the Zebra Pans. How I'm just not sure as there doesn't seem to be anything in the system for bikes. A Vidal Sassoon moment from the Blonde White Lady me thinks. Hey it worked and were off down the road heading out towards the coast.

Yeah it's as hot as it's ever been but to be honest my heads in the bottoms of my boots. Just not funny the only upside is we're out of town and rolling.

Things do get a bit easier over the next few days. I kinda get the hang of the Suicide Shifter and apart from the corrugations, the trail is easy enough. Apple Pie at Moose's Place in Solitaire. Cold Drinks in the StarWars Cantina. Ok just a roadside cafe that resembles something out of Star Wars. Strange looking Pod like buildings camouflaged by their rocky surrounding. But it did give us some of the best nights camping out.

That ever changing light bringing a multitude of photo opportunities our way. The desert moonscape constantly changing as the light builds or fades. Dropping blankets of colour over the mountains throughout the course of the day. When the moon does make his appearance your amazed once more. The stars appearing one by one to decorate the curtain of night. A gift from Africa.

Leaving the mountains behind us in the morning we're heading out towards the Zebra Pans. With the horizon stretching out all around us there's real feeling of nothingness. Not much Bush, Not many animals, not much of anything apart from the Giant Sand Dunes of Naukluft, Stretching out into the distance.

Aptly named the pans, as the only thing out there are a few scattered Zebra. Oh and a standing stone proclaiming the Tropic of Capricorn. Mmm… a mile stone really. We're on the move… but we are heading for the desert camp at Homeb. We're not sure what is waiting for us but we do know this is one of the few official places to stay.

There's not much on the horizon bar a few rocky outcrops. Eyes deceiving us me thinks, as a darker line crosses in front of us and as we get nearer we do see the track heading down into a canyon. Relief as there the odd tree and more and more bush. Maybe there is a good place to camp.

A community campsite with virtually no amenities but what it lacks in comfort and style, it makes up for in Wow!.. Cool place to sit out the heat of the day in the shade… Not much of a community really, just a few wooden built houses for the goat herders and their families but they had the beauty that was this oasis in the desert. Well cool.

[Video No. 11: **Zebra Pans**]

Heading out on the 4x4 track in the morning, I for one was feeling pretty pleased!. Pleased my foot had stood up to the challenge that is. Chuffed we had made the effort to go on and not call it a day… Time to treat ourselves in Swakopmund, I think we've earned it this time.

A few days to resupply and check over the bikes. A visit to the last Yamaha shop I think I'll see for a while. Chill, WiFi catchup and I might even have time to get a haircut. Oh and we did treat ourselves to dinner in a real pub. Happy days...

Kaokoland

Out of Swakopmund and into the desert. Well up the coast road first. The Skeleton Coast. A windy affair but what do you expect and you can understand how it received its name. Shipwrecks by the dozen litter the coast line as we push north.

Stop at one of them was enough though. A rusting hulk of what used to be an Angolan Trawler apparently. There's a couple of guys sitting there trying to sell desert gem stones to any tourist that passes by. Not for us, we're bad tourists I'm afraid but we had a chat and a photo shoot with them next to their improvised skeleton in the sand. Everyone needs a gimmick, no? These guys had come from a village up north. Not exactly seeking fame and fortune, just a living as times are hard.

Easy life in the desert and a few nights under the stars once more. The Trick-cyclist doing more than her fair share of the work as I hobbled on. I do try to make adjustments to the steering on Shaun. I had repacked the headstock with grease back in town. Thought that was that to be honest but maybe I just didn't tighten it enough. Oops! Tools out and put it right.

Sitting under the moon, its easy conversation from travels that had come before. We both gave accounts of our previous Elephant encounters. Heidi had seen so much from her last African Adventure. Remembering oh so many as she cycled through Botswana. Me not so much. Once and once only I have. A visit to Sri Lanka so many years before. The bus transfer from the airport had to give way to jumbo trotting down the street. Logging chains on and pilot on-board he really did have the right of way. Just wanted to see him in a more natural environment. Dreamlands always good though.

I thought the Zebra Pans were good but this place took on a whole new look. Still as hot and just as beautiful. That constant changing light thing.

We'd love to see the free roaming desert elephant and at the same time hope we don't run straight into him. Not known for their politeness. Rather on the aggressive side it's said. We'll have to wait as that night's treat was Rutting Springbok and a whole herd of Gemsbok in the riverbed. Hard to count but maybe 40–50.

Plenty of elephant dung as the big guy has left his calling card all over the place. To be honest it did get my heart racing when we were pitching the tent on the far side of the riverbank knowing he'd been around and about fairly recently. Pitched we did and managed to sleep for a bit. Up in the morning with the lark looking forward to what was to come.

Up the track nice and early was the idea. Plenty more calling cards and one almighty Gemsbok (Oryx).

We almost missed the tracks that lay before us as we were distracted by the Gemsbok. The Big Guy had been here and maybe only hours before and was heading the same way as us. Said our farewells to the Gemsbok and off up the hill we went crossing even more tracks. Heart really pumping know. We could see a thin line of green vegetation ahead. A sure sign of water? Hey! The Big Guys got a thirst too. More tracks than we can imagine but no Elephants. It looks like a regular spot for him. Plenty of calling cards and what looks like a hide up on the hill.

Just wish we could have hung around and use it.

There's no Dunkers left not much of anything left. Well not enough for another day. We needed to pass through some sort of village or town for resupply. Only 4 days from Swakopmund but we can't carry much more and be comfortable.

Our meeting with the Free Roaming Desert Elephants will have to wait for another day. We'll meet soon enough I'm sure of it. I'd rather it be on good terms. The thought of seeing them out here is more appealing than the game reserve. I don't know why. Un-chained, Un-tamed, It just is.

Anyway, there will be other chances as we go back off track towards Puros. The DeathZone that is the desert towards Orumpembe. It's not really the DeathZone but not much lived out there.

More sand than I would like on route to Puros but we would be treated to one of the death-zones very best before the end of the day.

Through the dry river bed and up the other side. A whole Tower of Giraffes, a family group of 20 maybe 30 of them. Just an awesome sight. Are they just a freak of nature? Or one of Mother Nature's best! To me one of the most spectacular animals on the planet. They were a bit dusty, dirty and a bit skinny but truly beautiful. They'd adapted to their surroundings and were right at home. Their movement something to behold. Legs, body, head all out of sync but strangely efficient galloping up to 50kph. Crazy speeds for something so out of the ordinary. A wonderful creature…

Back down the track and not what we really wanted to see as we know we're not making Puros. We are ready to wild-camp in the bush.

Paw Prints. Yip, Lion!

Move on and find another spot. Down by another dried up riverbed and it's time for us to stop. Can't keep pushing it for that's when accidents happen. Pick your best spot and go with it. Set up the trail camera and see what uses the riverbed on a night time.

Not much. Well not according to the camera.

A few deer antelope types through the night then maybe only an hour before sun up a very agitated beast in the riverbed. Round and around in circles this way and that. Confusion reigned as he didn't know which way to go. He made a choice. The wrong choice as we herd the squeal of something getting got. We looked at each other. No words were needed but eventually whispers came from beside me. "What do you think it was?"

I didn't answer for a moment as I'm sure she really knew the answer to her own question. "Don't know but I'm not going out to check!"

We lay there trying to block out the thought of what happened.

Just hope it's true what they say about the tent. The cats see it as an inanimate object and don't register it as a snack-box!

Morning tea. Trying to forget what went before. Wondering if we should have a second cuppa. So glad we did as we sat on the river bank one of the best things ever. A lone Giraffe wanders through the riverbed. GobSmacked!

We sat there staring for a bit but sneaked around the tent out of view so as to get our cameras.

Back on the bank before the main viewing. Not the gangly mis-shapen creature we had seen the night before but something more poised just going about his day. He's just effortlessly gliding by. Not in a hurry in fact stopping momentarily to turn his head and check us out before gliding off on his way. A wonderful moment that I don't think has ever happened to me before... Maybe it has but not for a while. Ha-De-Da...

How do you top that? I'm not sure you can. We just got on with our day. A trip to the Man United Mini Mart at Puros puts another smile on my face before the endless rough track of the DeathZone. Not even painted in the Man-Utd red but some strange green colour. Is this the same Red Devils from home?

A long day. In fact a bloody long day. Don't think I've been so far out on the edge for a while. Sure I've been privileged enough to have been to so many places but this was on the edge. Not much lived out here. Bugga I'm not sure much could survive out here. There's nothing. No vegetation, just nothing but rock sand and track. Not much of a track either but enough for you to follow.

We kept moving along stopping as we went taking pictures as the ever changing light changed our surrounding. It never made it more habitable though.

There's a pot of gold at the end of every rainbow. It came in the shape of a little store in Oropembe. Albeit in the strange shape of a rather large African women in the most unexpected dress. I say dress but I say it a bit tongue in cheek. Brightly coloured dress with tartan apron and cow horned shaped hat that wouldn't look out of place from years gone by. A real throwback to the Victorian days. Didn't understand the Bantu she spoke to me… Coke break and it never tasted so good… Not for long as we wanted a better camp spot. That never ending search for Bush Camping Valhalla, so we push on.

Another set of cat tracks and move on even more (sleepless night ahead me thinks). Another dried up riverbed and time to settle on the far bank. Check for tracks and pitch. Set up the trail camera. Not having much luck with this. But I'll trade that for a peaceful night in the bush as that is what it turned out to be.

Mother Nature can't spoil you every night or breakfast time.

More supplies required so into town proper before the challenge of the Van Zyl's Pass.

It's the only way we think we could succeed. Ditch some of our kit, just lighten the load and give it a go.

So many people would give advice about the pass. Well, brag about how hard it was for them and warn you off from going. You might not make it!

We watched a few videos and it did look pretty tuff in places (amazing thing YouTube, just not always helpful). We were starting to think, we wouldn't actually be able for it?

Mr Yamaha back in Swakopmund made up our minds to be honest. Chatting on the street checking out our bikes. He looked at Heidi and told us not too. I saw the look on her face and I didn't need to ask again. Auld Fart!

Amazing how people want to express an opinion or give advice before first asking, have you done anything like it before. Sound familiar?

Hey I'm no different.

When I met Heidi in Mongolia a few years back it's exactly what I did. She was going one way on her bicycle and me the other on my

Tiger. I tried to give her all sorts of details and help before asking her what she had done before. A more experienced traveller I've yet to meet. One with some balls. Hence I knew what was in store as Mr Yamaha doubted her without knowing her. Bring it On!

Bring it On!

Up the boring road to Okangwati. Not the prettiest but it's a means to an end. Fuel from a plastic bottle and out into the bush heading for Van Zyl's. The track twisted all ways and I'm sure it was written all over my face how I wasn't coping with the deep sand. Not! To put it mildly but things did get better as the trail gained some height and climbed into a more rocky section but time was catching us as we neared the pass. Only 10km to go but we just had to stop. Both of us were tired and I'm sure that's what caused Heidis off on the last climb. Take 5, but the sight of my 1st baobab tree was enough for us to abandon the bikes and go climbing.

[Video No. 12: **My First Baobab Tree**]

Very cool indeed. It's a strange creation. The biggest trunk you've ever seen with much shorter spindly limbs than you would imagine. But this was a beast with room for two. By the time we stopped being children it really was time to camp. Hey everyone should climb a tree now and then but into the bush once more!. A faint serenade from the last village we passed as we slipped off to dreamland.

Van Zyl's

Up and at it! We left the Baobab behind and went in search of Van Zyl's.

We found him soon enough. Not hard to miss as we reached the top of the pass. Two Ford Rangers there before us.

A well retired group of four making the most of life and far better for it. They didn't care how long it took them. But they were well capable and up for the challenge. Quite eager to help fellow travellers like us. Fellow bikers they were and knew how hard it was for us but they weren't daft enough to bring their BMWs. The little bike is just what's needed for this. We still got off and helped each other in places. Sometimes you just need that safe and steady hand beside you. More a confidence boost as I never needed to help Heidi too much. She's growing in confidence and more than capable.

Pictures galore and down to the view point. What was all the fuss about? Break time and a cuppa was in order or is there a sting in the tail.

Oh yes. Best part of an hour later and the 4x4s have caught up and started on the last pitch. Oopsi! Up on 2 wheels as the trail plunges off the edge but they're not really fazed. They wait a moment and let us through once more but we wait at the bottom. Comrades in arms as we toast Van Zyl's. I couldn't really stomach the beer that was on offer (yeah I know a refusal doesn't happen very often) but their friendship was appreciated.

They were off soon enough leaving use to our sandy nightmare. The hard rocky footing left on the pass behind us. Or was that just me as once more Heidi shot off leaving me to pin-ball down the track. Hours later that sandy hell threw me over the bars or was it JackSparrow protesting about his workload. Anyways mutiny it was as he refused to play the game. Sent me flying or sailing over the handlebars. Oops sand then sky followed by, Quick hit the kill switch and lay back to check out the sky once more. Not for long as that sweat stench of unleaded filled my nostrils. Bugga fuel pouring out everywhere. Couldn't pick it up quick enough. Ah he is digging his heels in. The side stand is pointing straight down, firmly planted in the sand.

The spring is missing and it makes me wonder when it jumped overboard. As we crashed or was the instigator? Digging in and send us bunny hopping from the rear. Who knows but my foot complains at the effort. I may have my bike boots on and got rid of my crutches back in Sesfontein but my foot is far from full fitness. Something I was to regret later as I struggled to get me boots off.

We zigzagged across Marienfluss before cutting our way through the bush once more. Ok! the track was there but not always the straight line that was on the map. Constantly changing direction as the tide changed the shifting track. The sand would make it impossible and so a new track would start where ever it could. Sometimes many side by side.

Time to camp but there is no markings on the track and yet another camp missed. Map, track or dodgy satnav who knows but we missed it, but the bush is good enough. Just the prospect of taking my boots off that prayed on my mind.

As I thought. A tuff day and my foot had worked harder than I wanted it too. Took more of the pain killers before I went down that road. But it did come off. Albeit with a squeal. I'm not proud as it hurt like hell. By rights I should have rested it more but sometimes you just got to take your chances when opportunities arise in front of you. Who knows, we might never be back in Namibia.

We enjoyed our evening, Heidi purring like a kitten through the night as we feel asleep well contented. She's amazing when I think of it… the days ride was pretty full on but were both still smiling…

"Morning Blossom!" Up the track early was the plan. We still had that same smile on, but we were both tired. Yesterday was full-on but more from the dozen or so days hard riding across the desert really! An accumulation of hard days all taking their toll.

100km to Etanga. At least we could get there. Water? Even a shop maybe?

The day past with ever tiring bikers at the helm. We were glad to see the village ahead.

Kids in the track asking if they can help?

We're looking for the campsite.

Only one spoke English which was enough.

He persuaded us to go to church. Which to be fair was trying to be the community campsite. It just wasn't there yet. Not finished but we or a least I'd had it for the day.

The church was nothing but a frame with a thatched roof and one small room in concrete block. But the cross on the roof gave it away. There was no doubting whose house it was.

A new first for me as we pitched the tent where the congregation should have been and the kids ran off, well dragged Heidi off to fetch water.

Heidi gave them her camera to take some pictures as we sorted ourselves out. Result as they took pictures of each other that we just couldn't have asked for. More climbing trees and Smiling face. Posing as Usain Bolts. It's all good!

Tea time. And they watched as we unpacked our stove. Standing back as it burst into life. Not many campers visit these parts I think. A cuppa and pass out the eat-some-mor Dunkers we'd been saving. Couldn't help but notice their manners in receiving and sharing out of the biscuits. Hey I wish all kids were like this. Refreshing more than the tea.

Any doubts about staying were dispelled as they headman or village chief came around to introduce himself. Basago my English interpreter immediately took a more respectful stance with the headman. Not that he had been anything but friendly with me but this 14 year old certainly knew his place in the village. Whispering his name in my ear. Imcoachya.

It turned out we had missed his father the church pastor as he was off into town some 100km away to see a doctor but it was all settled. We were to stay here in the church with our new friends as protectors. The chief went on his way. More handshakes and bows. Mmm… my 1st chief.

Cheekily or not we sent a couple of the kids to the shop for Coke. Two bottles. Before you knew it they were back. One for the kids to share and one for the big kids to share. Fare deal I thought, and yet again pleased to see them share it out amongst themselves so very equally. Five of them but it was a big bottle so all was good

A game of footie with a burst baw but they didn't seem to mind. Hey what you gonna do. None of them had shoes never mind a spare ball. All good fun though. Me, I took some video and played it back to them. Can't believe there was 4 clones of Messi on that churchyard pitch.

Only one girl and that does throw me a little. They seem to run around in little shorts/pants and nothing else. Stick with it the rest of their lives as they hang on to the traditional Himba ways. But the boys don't. As modern or as western as you want and that starts early. Couldn't figure it out.

But the boys treated her well and share the biscuits and Coke with her before she left for where ever home was.

Good nights were exchanged as the older kids walked the younger ones home.

Not much time had passed before I heard. Jimi Jimi. We're back and off to bed…

No pun intended but feeling blessed as I lie in my tent, inside the church. Soothing sounds on the wind of the women folk of the village singing their traditional songs.

Jimi Jimi, Are you awake? Our hosts were!

Up and tea for us all. Not sure what they would normally have in the morning. My guess would be nothing. But with only 2 mugs the kids shared one and the big kids shared the other one. But there was enough rusks for all to dunk. Getting used to this dunking business.

Packed our gear and the boys approached us with a pumpkin. A gift from them. Heart wrenching as I knew they hadn't much of anything to spare. We declined. No room to carry it was our excuse.

Before we packed the bikes it was the churchyard Grand Prix. Helmets for the kids as I took them on the back of my bike around the churchyard one by one. Each taking it in turn to photograph or video with our cameras. Amazed at the care they took with them, putting the straps around there neck every time.

But before long it was time to go.

We Gave Basago some money as a gift to the chief of the village for allowing us to stay. More than it would have cost in any campsite but it was worth every penny.

Needless to say I was blown away by it all as my thoughts drifted back and forth across the previous days. Hard to concentrate on the road into town.

The people here have a hard life but a respect for each other which allows them to hold their heads high. The hand waving never stopped and the kids were always smiling.

Not always what you find when you get to the town.

Opuwa

We needed a few days to take stock of it all, totally blown away by the last few days. Many ups and downs and a realisation. In the grand scheme of things, we're doing alright! Maybe if I can put the Mr Handy messenger thingy to one side we just might manage to go the distance…

Swartzboy

There are a few days left in Namibia. Time for Epupa Falls on the Kunene River. An easy couple of days that's for sure. Ones that were forced on us with fatigue if I'm honest. Many days in the saddle. Sometimes you just got to take a day off. So we did nothing.

We were to follow the river east to Oshakati and sort ourselves out for crossing the border in to Angola… More easy days and a smile along the way.

Swartzboy. I'm not sure we had an actual conversation, just a one sided bullet-point version of his life. Made me laugh though…

Jake-Jactques Kapika

He was Angolan
They were proud
They were always pleased to see us, pleased to see white people
No white people came here
This is your woman
You should stay
You look like good people
Brother and sister no?
You can marry my Sister
you can marry my brother
We need people to handle our diamonds
No black people can do it
We are stock piling them
No, my life follows a different path
Stay marry my sister.
No, Heidi wouldn't marry me then!
You should come back maybe 3 years
My father king of the Himba people
Brief Escape
Ah u stay
We need you white people
Water my 1st son will fetch it (not his son)
Give me $20
Buy me a beer
Not because I'm poor, but we are friends
Give me $10
He wasn't drunk he was punch drunk, a boxer
choppers
Must go, be safe
Heir to the thrown indeed
Giggle, oh we did but WTF!:-) Ha-De-Da…

Oshakati: Into town and everything that it had to offer. The glory that is Shoprite once more. Glorious!;-)

Picked up almost everything we thought we'd need for the road ahead. We even got a wallet full of dollars U.S. from the bank. For the just in case, and maybe a bit of money changing on the side.

Time to service the bikes but not everything checked out. Heidis been complaining that her steering feeling very vague. Mmm... she's not one for complaining but it seems to have gotten worse since we got to town.

I had checked it back in Namibia, even re-greased the headstock bearing but that was it. Bugga it scared me when I checked it. Test ride down the street and I was wondering how she actually manage to ride the thing.

No bike shop in town but we done our best to find a real mechanic. Just no joy. The Trick-cyclist would have to tough it out until Luanda.

We did meet some Brit Overlanders on the campsite. They were travelling south in their 4x4. Yip, sitting in the restaurant waiting on our pizza talking all things travel. They were telling their stories of the Congo and the Crazy-one is joining in. All good chat and then, "Are you the Heidi from the blog"? Cycling through Africa!

Heard all this before, No? They could tell almost all from Heidis last trip through Africa. It made us all laugh.

We had a magic time chatting and sharing our stories of all things Africa. A great couple but we were heading in different directions. Wished each other well and a quick photo session before we left. Hoped we'd meet again.

Hey it's Africa! But it's a small world too sometimes.

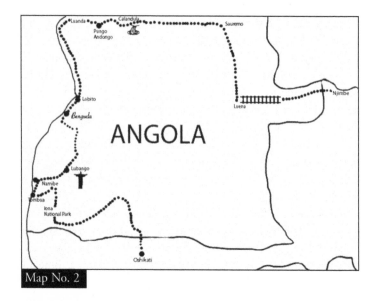

Map No. 2

9

The Angolan experience

Where do you start? At the border I suppose. Probably the most Mickey Mouse experience I've had in a long time. Border crossing shouldn't be like this. But Heidi just laughs and says welcome to Africa.

To be honest if we spoke Portuguese everything would have been different!

Not much English to be found around the border post but plenty of fixers self-appointing themselves as your personal helper and translator. What a joke!

The whole experience would have been easier if they weren't there. Don't know where the security was. Just mystified me. Anyway after three and a half hrs. a trip to the ATM, the Chinese photo-print shop and much huffing and puffing we were let loose.

Not a great start but we were in and on our way.

Not much progress down the road I must admit but when we did stop the people were friendly. We were looking for somewhere to camp. Directed to the local police. Mmm…

They were friendly enough and with Heidis Spanglish it was park your bike here and pitch your tent there. I must admit Heidis Spanglish is much better than my Portuguess. They even opened the commandant's personal bathroom for the lady.

A true first for me. Well my first voluntary night in the nick. But we won't go there!

The Dollar is King

All good and out on the road in the morning. Bike spares shop for oil and maybe a spring for my side stand. Found out the Portuguese name for the spring. Moller, but didn't find one. Did some money changing instead.

Couldn't get my head around the money thing for a while but you got more bang for your Buck on the street. The US Dollar is King.

All the rich kids want Dollars but the banks have none so the moneymen on the street give you a fantastic rate and sell them on. Basically the economy is fucked and the price of oil just isn't helping. Three or four times more for us than what we'd get at the bank.

The war had a lot to answer for! Angola is a former Portuguese colony and the Portuguese held on that bit longer than most of the colonial powers. Something which they all did in some way or another. If they all had planned exit strategies for management and self-rule after the day of independence. The whole of Africa would be in a better state all round. All the Portuguese left was a power vacuum and unrest for the next 40 years.

But enough of that there's riding to be done…

A Russian made T-55 at the side of the road. A stark reminder of this country's recent and turbulent past. A quick photo shoot and try not to mention the war.

Turn off the main road after our Cahama fuel stop. Extra needed for the ride through the Iona National Park. We just wouldn't make it if the trail turns too soft and sandy. So plastic Coke bottles filled with fuel in my water carriers. Serves a purpose, but we decant into the tank as soon as we can.

We talked about the trail and came to the decision. If there were recent tyre tracks then they were ok to use.

What with an estimated 20 million mines laid throughout the recent conflict, we would err on the side of caution. Halo Trust one of the agencies dealing with the mine situation proclaimed they won't reach the government target of mine free by 2025. What a thought!

Anyways the trail was awesome so we carried on. It just got smaller and less travelled but never really disappeared.

The locals were friendly enough which was a bonus as we don't speak the lingo. No need for my Portuguess either as the villagers spoke their own language. Herero or Himba tribal stuff here. But they were cool with us pitching our tent next to the village water pump.

It did take a bit of time to explain ourselves but eventually we just popped it up and gave the thumbs up sign. All was good with them.

They stood around watching us playing with our camping gear. They soon got bored and carried on with their daily chores so then we watch the half-naked women of the village, pump water. Mind boggling and cross eyed:-) They slinked off to their village and we enjoyed the sunset and a cuppa. Awesome night's sleep to go with it.

Up early as everyone who was anyone in this village came by to say goodbye, or just watch and laugh as I tried to get water from the pump. Women's work it seems as none of the guys would give me a hand. Not the done thing it seems. But the interaction was fantastico (my Portuguess word for really cool people).

We hit the trail once more. There are a few villages along the way but none of any real size. Everyone has a surprised look on their face as we go by but most wave after their initial shock. It's all good, there's shock but no horror. No one sees us as a threat to their peaceful way of life.

We're heading for Iona and mostly, the trail is good riding with the occasional dried riverbed come sand pit but its good enough. It was still tough and the odd rocky section kept you on your toes. Small villages and even an odd ageing church along the way. Not all of them inhabited or in use anymore, maybe a sign of the times but plenty of goats either side of the trail. A good sign of no land mines. Just as well...

Stopped in the final riverbed of the day and it looks good so we decide it's our next camping spot. Quick scrape of the sand to rid ourselves of all things spikey. Inflatable mattresses while comfortable and light, there's certain drawbacks!

Throwing aside some of the debris before settling down. There's an old piece of rope in my flop down zone. Rusty, brown with white climber's style colourful kinda thing. As I reach out to move it on but instantly I jump back. Not a piece of rope. Bugga!

Heart in the mouth for a moment as I realise exactly what this little wiggly thing is. Snake!

Can't believe I was about to pick it up. We hadn't seen any since back in Underberg, South Africa. Believe me we had seen enough back then. Boomslang hiding out in the bush next to our tent, the crazy one stepping over a Rinkhals when we were hiking. Any of them would have sent you to hospital. Now this!

I'm not sure what it was but it does focus my attention for a while. Maybe a Horned Adder! Mmm…

Wilderness! There's no such thing as the Wilderness!

Apart from the odd disused village we've virtually seen no one all day. Then a man on horseback goes by and waves. A while later he drives a herd of cows back the other way and waves again. Surely that's it?

No! Donkeys everywhere, crying all night. Just where did they all come from. No sleep for the wicked it seems, just wonder what I've done in my previous life?

Iona village wasn't very far down the track and came quickly. Quick chat with the local constabulary. Shocked to see us me thinks! They filled up our water bottles and asked the usual questions but all was good. Their gossip for the day and we said our goodbyes. We did bump into the local bigwig on the way out of town. Ok still village size but bigger than anywhere we had ridden through for a while.

He too was a bit shocked surprised and excited all rolled into one. Stopped us and asked more of the usual questions. Not sure many tourists come down this track then, but he did wish us well. Pleased to see us I'm sure.

The scenery just kept getting better and better. Bloody awesome to be honest. The light changes throughout the day, changed the trail at every turn through the mountains. Not much wildlife! A few Dik-Dik and the odd Springbok but that was ok this place sold it to me on looks alone. I took more video here than most other trails.

We pushed further north through more open and golden plains but never tired of it. Then probably the biggest herd of Springbok we'd seen anywhere. A bit skittish I must admit but not many bikes or cars come through here I bet. We spent what seemed forever watching them bounce from one side of the track to the other. We tried not to startle them too much but didn't succeed. We eventually stuttered past.

The long grass turned every shade of gold you could imagine. Some of the best kilometres we've ridden I'm sure and yeah more video.

The golden Grasslands do eventually come to an end as we start to meander through the first of the approaching rocky outcrops. Who would have guessed there's a sting in the tale? Yeah, we should have learned by now. As we are confronted with a river crossing. But more surprising than that was the park entry kiosk on the other side of the river.

Mmm… paying on the way out? New one on me. This journey is full of firsts!:-) Signboard list the sponsors and donors helping to put the park back on the map. Just hope they get there.

It was getting long in the day and we were trying to make it to an old elephant hunters lodge. Alvaro Bautistas place. So it said in the guide book. He must have been thrashing his Aprilia in that weekends MotoGP as the gates were securely closed. A big pull on the outrageously large doorbell but no answer. It was another night in the desert for us.

Probably better as we had the best of sunsets and a fabulous night sky. Full of the stars we never really see at home. Probably one of the best camp spots we've ever had. Peaceful? Sleeping under the stars never felt so good.

Here Kitty Kitty

Up with the howls and screams of what roams this place. Heidi thinks she's funny by mouthing. "Here kitty kitty kitty" something she has done many a time. She soon sucked back into silence as they got closer and louder. Seemed like they had surrounded us at one point. Be careful of what you wish for eh! The Crazy-one not so crazy as she's was struck silent by the howls.

Whatever they were they passed us by and we enjoy the rest of our morning. Tea & Dunkers. WooHoo! Simple things for simple people.

There was still more trail to be ridden so saddle up. More sand I'm afraid. Just the pits. My bike just doesn't seem to cope with it. Frustrating as Heidi sails past with ease even with the vague feeling in her steering. This just sucks. Definitely looking for a bike mechanic soonest, there must be something to make it handle the soft stuff better.

Anyway get on with it. It can't last forever. But it felt like it.

Soon the sand faded and so did the feeling. Just get to the road and things will be good.

The SatNav showed the trail running through the middle of the lake. Nope! Not wet so, something's changed. The lay of the lake or just the water level?

Anyways we hit the road and turned for town. Tombwa.

Bugga it's Sunday. Why does that always happen?

As always nothing's open on a Sunday, but a quick look around town for some fuel. After 500km of off-road I really didn't have much left. The curse of getting bogged down in the extra soft sand, spinning the rear and slipping the clutch.

Escape back to the desert for our night's camp spot. It looked more like a quarry to be honest! Some earth had definitely been moved around here. Road works me thinks. The fact there was an old Cuban underground bunker nearby we weren't convinced of the landmines situation. But there had been some serious earth movers around here.

Peace and a couple of beers from Tombwa. For a Sunday it had done good. Our first Cuca Beers in Angola. A bit of a wash before dark and settle down for the evening. Not sure about washing her feet though as she asks me for a hand. Treats me like her personal slave...

Traffic Buffer in South Africa
Night Watchmen in the bush
Mechanic when it's not working
Mule when there's extra to be carried
Minesweeper when it's dodgy
Now This!

Roped into massaging them on occasion but my list of chores does seem to be growing. Big smile as she proclaims "there's a reason why I brought you to Africa"... Beginning to wonder...

Big smiles as the ride to the coast was what we had hoped for and a whole lot more. What a Ride!

Christ The Redeemer

Up the road to Namibe and Shoprite. All the goodies we had been craving.

Jackets off as we left the coast behind us and turned inland. The roads the pits in places and a pleasure to ride in others but you have to concentrate. You can't really see the beauty of the landscape for the heat haze but you know it's out there. The silhouettes of Monster Mountains through the glare gives you a glimpse of what hides out here.

The Leba Pass sneaks up on us. Maybe not as big as the alpine passes of Europe, but the Stelvio of the south. Switchback after switchback decorated in grafeetie (Modern day bushmen you think?) at almost every turn. Not that you could take time to check out the wall art as the turns came thick and fast. The temperature rising as you climb on and on. As in all the pleasures in life it was over all too quick as we take the final turn to the cafe at the top. Time for a Coke and a reflection of what was. Well cool!

Time is getting on though, so it's more miles before camping but a real campsite this time. Sort of! Campsite on a farm but we have it all to ourselves which was good as we needed the rest. Remember all the pleasures in life thing? Gone in a flash and back on the road in the morn.

Lubango and Christ The Redeemer.

The monument sits looking over the city with a commanding view. Not quite Rio but still impressive. Apparently there are three monuments. Brazils Rio de Janeiro, here in Lubango and Lisbon in Portugal. I bet the others don't have bullet holes like this one. But the big guy survived the war so maybe there is hope for Angola too.

[Video No. 13: **7 Days in Angola**]

10

Hey Amigos

Down into town and the relative comforts of what we would call posh, Casper Lodge. All be it camping in our tent in the garden.

Some shopping and some internet. I wish I had stopped with the Internet and left the walk around town to be honest. The foot not too strong yet and it hurts like hell. In fact, wish I had my crutches back. I know someone in the makeshift clinic in Sesfontain will be benefiting from them. Just might regret giving them away so soon. A day of rest in the garden goes down a treat.

Up early and move through town with the morning madness, for it is madness! No time to relax or let your guard down. But I'm sure they do a better job at avoiding us than we think, so we manage to escape soon enough. Heading for Benguela and Lobito on the coast. We're not gonna make it in a day but for a change we get our heads down and put in some miles.

Stop at the village shop to share a Coke and ask about camping possibilities. No English but Heidis Spanglish gets us a pitch in the shops back yard. More good people that just want to see you alright. Starting to like this place.

Up in the morning and say our goodbyes. What can I say? Just nice people. Shop keeper never asked for anything but eventually excepted my token gift. Cervesa, with a beer hand gesture. He got the message. Good guy…

Benguela awaits us so get on with it. It didn't take long to be fair. We were there for a late breakfast or early lunch.

A nice feel to the place. Easy going seafront with good places to eat. Well, it was where we stopped. Very relaxed we trundled along the seafront out of town towards Lobito. A bigger town with a bigger reputation. Didn't really get to where we were going. Zulu, a sea front bar that allows camping. A truck stops us. Where you going he asks. Didn't get the answer out when he asks the next. Where are you staying? Didn't answer that one either. He insist we stay at his other bar. Bar Alfa. Turns out Hugo runs both these family owned bars.

Pitch your tent here park your bike there. Sound familiar? Starting to really like Angola.

Tent up on the beach, beer in hand and catch up on the world. Late Lunch is on its way. What a place. Well cool.

Hugo knew everyone. He was leaving for the capital early in the morning to attend some biker meet. A big thing for him as he ran biker gatherings here and their club was growing. But before he left he introduced us to what seemed like everyone in Lobito. Hand never stopped shaking, my glass never empty.

Great night but it's gonna hurt in the morning. Wow! It did. Can't remember going to bed. No shower and no dinner. Not a good combination. But a weekend of rest on the beach. What a Life!

Luanda

Up and pack up our gear. Well almost. A false start I'm afraid. Unpack as we're still knackered. Only one more day.

We did eventually get going and took the smallest road to the capital. Nothing exceptional I'm afraid. It just served that purpose. Across the Kwanza River and that was the highlight. Well almost. Stopped for some lunch at the side of the road and a truck stops. Reverses about 100m to park beside us. A biker no less doing his day job. You know The Amigos da Picada he asks.

Oh yeah!

Do you know Lilio? We ask.

El Presidenti!

That's the one... Lilio was the one who organised the letter of invitation to assist in our visa application. A friend of a friend who we had never met but yeah he was president of the biggest biker club in Angola and it was him we were off to meet. Small world as seconds later we were speaking to him on your man's phone and organised meeting up that afternoon.

Down the yacht club. Not what I expected from a biker but hey! while in Rome?.

Lilio had sorted everything out. Club Nautico will let us pitch our tent in the grounds for free. Awesome! Armed security guards and all. More awesome!

Sorted ourselves out and a snooze in our tent before meeting the guys down town. Or so we thought as. Hello hello. I'm Andrew. Fancy a beer? Adrian said you'd be coming to town. Who's Adrian? Bugga the beer in Lobito had a lot to answer for as that is where we met Adrian and he got on his phone, let Andrew know we were heading to town. Andrew and his family made us welcome and an offer of using their house if we wanted. Wi Fi, hot shower, air conditioned and a washing machine. Didn't need our arms twisted to except that one but not tomorrow, we had chores to do and bikes to get serviced some how.

Into town to meet the Amigos. Great bunch of guys. Really made us welcome and basically sorted out most of our chores. Well bike wise anyways. Bike mechanic tomorrow morning at the meeting place, outside the scrapyard. All our oils on order. What a day. What a night. Didn't need any rocking that evening.

Up with a text from Andrew reminding us of the washing machine and Wi-Fi offer. But around the Amigos meeting place to get the bike serviced. Yip, Amigos were there to help and the mechanic turns up on his Chinese scooter. Apprentice holding on tightly to the toolbox. Portuguess on hand and plenty of hand signals helps us get through the work list. Simple tasks but I wanted someone to check what I'd been doing to bikes the last few months. Oil change and the normal basics along with valve clearances and a look at my front end. Change the fork oil and find different quantities in either fork leg. Well that won't help but feeling better after the change. Heidis flat spot on the steering turned out to be my over tightening of the headset. Oops, I won't be admitting to that one! You live and learn. Good job she could ride around that vague feeling in her steering. All done and off for fish dinner with the guys. Oh and a few beers. I use the word awesome far too much but what can you say about a bunch of guys who just dropped everything to escort us around town and sorted out all our admin well almost all... They don't do the washing machine bit...

Andrews's driver turned up in the morning for us. What luxury. Beautiful house at our disposal. Washing all done and dried, shower, shave and Wi-Fi to catch up with the world. FaceTime for the lucky ones but we do ask to come back the following day. Nannies birthday. She's 99 and deserves a happy birthday.

No problems.

Sunset down the beach with our new friends and family. An early night and make some plans...

FaceTime for the birthday girl which was cool. Nice to see her smile. More dodgy money dealings and the last of our shopping. Meet up with the guys for beers. Cool day.

Can't fault them as even more Amigos turn up that night. Never thought I'd feel so welcome in the scrapyard. Snack bar outside with beer on tap. What more could you ask for? In a word nothing... Never felt so welcome. Anywhere...

Breakfast with George our host and leader of the local chapter. Can't thank him enough. Our stay in Luanda gave us so many new friends.

VISA clock ticking though, so we're heading east. Glad to get out of the city to be honest. Apart from our new friends it's too crazy for me. But the further east we go the going gets easier.

Dondo at the wrong time of day. Not long till dark. Ask the coppers for camping options and it turns out there's a guesthouse. Still not really paid for a bed yet so why not. It turned out to be cool. Out for fish dinner in the swankiest place in town. Tough life on the road eh! It wasn't that swanky but good fish.

Did I say we don't treat ourselves too often! Life's treating us kindly!

Pungo Andongo. Apparently the black rocks stopped Livingstone in his tracks on his transcontinental crossing so many years ago. Maybe he just needed to rest on his journey across the continent. We were intrigued and curious as I'm sure he was too, but for us they made for a safe campsite and some cool pictures. Solid rock base. No landmines here!

A day at the Calandula Falls. Well lunch and a walk about. The falls speak for themselves. A flood of thundering, rushing water with a wet wall of spray to match any waterfall you're ever going to visit. Just not much in the way of tourism out here I'm afraid. The Angolan people are missing a trick me thinks. I really hope they get things back track. So much potential. Two beautiful spots right in the heart of Angola, within striking distance of the capitol.

We keep heading east. A quick glimpse of Queen Ngjinga statue in Melange. A Warrior Queen of old, She may have had some impressive victories against the Portuguese but not that impressive!

A crumbling lump of rock if I'm honest. Visit the super-market and out of town with the more impressive Nginga branded bag of coffee.

Small town people us.

The shop keeper very welcoming. Free Coke but we share. These people don't have much! Ask about camping and he takes us to the police station. Hey they're cool. Put us in their next door neighbours garden. Ok they did ask. But always cool. Chill with them. A couple of beers and some dinner. Entertainment for the locals as the crowd around our impromptu campsite grows.

Still loving Angola.

[Video No. 14: **Blazing Saddles**]

The road goes further east. APCs along the verge. More reminders of their recent history. Not serviceable but more a blank canvas for the graffiti artist.

The road's surface isn't perfect but there's not many gear changes. I've been using my Suicide Shifter since Windhoek and it really is time I used the up-shift on my own. My foot was heeling and I was hobbling less and less, so I give it a go. Oh it hurts, I wasn't sure about it but you've got start somewhere.

East further east. The roads was becoming the pits. Full of potholes and broken bridges. I wonder why? Bailey Bridge replacements and a washing platform for the locals with the bombed out wreckage of the past. Not straying too far off the road here.

Towns and villages are becoming few and far between as the countryside opens up to show us those rolling fields that have so much potential for modern day farming. It's just not there yet. With the day drawing to an end we stop in the next village. We need somewhere to stay and ask for the Soba. Head guy or chief. He's welcoming and we can pitch next to his shop. All is good.

The kids all come to watch but soon get board of the strange white people. They don't do much! The men come and ask the questions that burn. The usual really, Where you from? Where you going? Are you Not Frightened? Then later the workers. The woman folk, coming around after making dinner but it was all good. The older kids do come back in those early evening hours but are soon chased by the soba. Shouting at the darkness he walks around his shop telling them what's what. Hey a good night's sleep.

He was gone in the morning but as I shake his wife's hand goodbye I slipped her some money and whisper gifty. Not much but every little helps. Made us feel better and I'm sure it helped a little. You gotta love Angola.

Day after day brought more of the same but we never seemed to tire of it. More villages and more police stations. We were made welcome and looked after wherever we stopped.

We did get stopped maybe 2 or 3 times every day at police check points but all was good. It's what they do. Nothing moves without them knowing it. Call me paranoid but being followed was never far from my mind. Too many coincidences and funny phone calls on our whereabouts by the communications officers. Secret police more likes! But coming out of a long civil war does this to you me thinks.

No harm done and I felt looked after. It was only the older policemen that put me on edge. The young ones were never brought up in the good old corruption days.

Only 2 crossed words in a month and one of them I let go as my fault. Nearly ran the check point. Didn't think he was gonna check my papers the other was just your average traffic cop. Cock! Even the immigration guys rolled their eyes at him and took me to one side muttered to each other and laughed. Traffic cops are the same the world over, who would have guessed it.

Saurimo, the hub for the diamond rich industries of eastern Angola. A posh hotel, well, posh for out here in the sticks. A stunning meal with an ice cold beer. It was a far cry from the roadside noodles and we deserved it. I'm sure I mention that before.

Turned south heading for the last real town on our route to the Frontera. Luena.

There are thousands of Chinese scooter in Angola and I said to myself long ago I wasn't gonna stop and fix them at the side of the road. We'd never make any progress. But you can't go by anyone with the dreaded P.......

Stopped and gave him a patch and me glue but the tube was dry and totally useless. Delving into her pack the Crazy-one takes control. Amazing to watch 4 African guys stand back and watch the woman do the work. Made me giggle, and I get my camera out. Great moments on the road.

A twist in the road and an old style Bailey bridge guarded at either end by tanks. Bugga me they should have been in the museum rather than out here. Russian T-34 me thinks and another stuck out in the field not a 100m away… Very curious.

More village life and another friendly welcome. We asked for the Soba but Ronda his wife took control. A lovely woman. Pictures with the kids always gets a smile and the barriers come down. Not that there was any really. The adults like to pose for their pictures. I get out my IPad and play the Tom & Jerry cartoons I had saved from YouTube. Just not sure what they thought but there's smiles all round. I'll keep my Mesi football videos for next time. Not so many football crazy kids in this family.

11
Jimbe Frontera

Luena. The last fuel stop and shop. Rubber glue. A chat with the local scooter crew. No English but hey, bikers are bikers. Photo shoot with them all. Except me as they were more interested in getting their picture taken with the Biker Chick. She might be my wife but they'll still chance their luck.

What you gonna do? Laugh it off and crack on. They were good lads really.

Out of town and head east once more. Follow the railway line for some of the 500km to the NJimbe Frontera.

Not the most scenic of rides and to be honest, a long day. The road went from bad to worse. No Tarmac and plenty of those giant dust bowl pot holes. Nothing exciting until we hit Smallville. It wasn't marked on my map. Cool guy in Justine at the town's water-pump. He was from Zambia and just wanted to say hello. He was working locally as a mechanic. He didn't think much of the road we were taking but he did give a good description of what was to come. Bugga!

Said our goodbyes and headed out of town and down the track, but not for long as the day was almost over. The next village was in sight and it's about that time.

We asked about camping and were directed to the house de Santos's. We did ask for the soba but 2 turned up. Not the sole chief of the village but rather the heads of the family and it seems there was more than one family.

Confusion reigns!

Not the best of conversations and with my non improving Portuguess, I was feeling helpless. I can feel the tension building as Heidi tries to answer all the questions. Just don't think they got what we wanted. Nothing!

Neither soba spoke any English but hey, that's not their fault. It was just so frustrating that we couldn't get through. We wanting nor needing nothing, other than to pitch our tent.

I could see the shorter of them getting shirty with those around him who tried to help. Hand slapping and handbags. His nose was out of joint as we could communicate with the circle around us but not him. There was both tension and anger. Not what we wanted at all.

The final straw was when cock-face kept shouting at Heidi. I could see the tears in her eyes and that was it. Stood up and gave it to him both barrels in English. Let's go...

The villagers that had gathered found their voice and let it be known that we were to stay. The loud mouthed soba was to be pushed out the meeting.

De Santos was brilliant. Not one to be pushed aside. She let him have it too.

She wanted us to stay and that was that. A strong woman. I think you need to be around here. Strong that is.

Things settled down and we pitched our tent. Tuna and noodles all done Heidi went for a lie down. I sat by the fire bucket which was put in front of the tent and answered all the questions our newly found interpreter had for me. Nothing new. Where you going? What's your job? Not sure they didn't think that we were looking for work in Angola. I was just about to call it a night when the Land Rover turned up. Nothing strange there but out jumped the Kalashnikov welding security dudes. Bugga not now.

Heidi Got up but there's no need the communications officer is with them and he speaks English as the local Commandanti only speaks Portuguese. Communication officer? More secret police me thinks. Phoned by cock-face no doubt.

Hey at least I could deal with this one. Not sure if he already had a Dossier on us. What with the amount of questions we've answered for communications officers along the way. Mmm…

He took my phone number and he gave me his email just in case I needed help. Not convinced about this one, he could answer more of his own question himself. Strange fish! Hey, maybe me being paranoid. The fact that my phone hadn't been turned on in months, inwardly made me smile. There's no chance we're staying in touch.

Sleep will help

Not sure what time everyone left but we were exhausted, truly done in. It didn't stop us getting up early as the crowd was gathering outside. Bleary eyed we have a quick cuppa and packed up.

It seemed the whole village except cock-face had come to say goodbye. Quick photo session and a gifty for DeSantos. Lovely lady. Gave her a big hug for good measure. I'm not sure she'll ever know exactly what she did for us. The kindness of strangers… makes us smile…

Down the track just keep going until we can be on our own.

Morning coffee at the side of the track. Chinese scooter goes by. He nearly breaks his neck turning around to stare.

Mmm… I entertain myself for the next half hour videoing the passer by and their reactions to the whities sitting drinking coffee at the side of the track. Laugh. We must have been in need of one. As one by one they wobble by and we giggle like a couple of school kids. Lekker eh.

They were all making their way from the Banana Festival me thinks. It was still going on when we rolled into town. Well at least some of the market stalls were trading. Half a dozen new tractors on display and people milling around everywhere. Busy Busy for this early that's for sure.

It's not for us and we move on. Too much authority after last night. The district governor was in town which explained the overkill in police presence.

Take A Look Up The Railtrack

Follow the train track once more. There's a definite water course at the side of us. Train track, road track and water. Mmm... It does seem like a drainage ditch but its dammed every so often like some sort of fish farm. People are tending it and fishing too. Something that we would see for the next 100 km with very few breaks in the Fish Farm drainage ditch.

It was like a real marshland type wilderness. More bird life along this stretch than we've seen in a long time. The riding became a pleasure too. The Chinese scooter line seemed to work best for us. The locals would use the foundation of the railway track to travel on instead of the totally unpredictable trail conditions. It was solid and the Chinese scooters left us a great line to follow. Awesome ride!

Lunch in the disused train station complete with bullet holes. Those telltale signs of war never really go away but we never stray too far. Peaceful times for us as we sit in the shade. The days ride was well cool especially after yesterday's shenanigans.

Luacano wasn't far so we pushed on. Fuel stop required if it's available.

Thankfully it was. Sitting at the side of the dirt road was a collection of wine bottles on top of an old oil drum. Strange vintage for anywhere else but here. Gasolina! At least we hoped it was. 16 of them. We'll take them all even at double the price of the forecourt. These will save us a journey into the town of Lual and a few km.

The crowd grows around us and we joke with the kids. I'm not sure I'm that funny but I get a few laughs.

[Video No. 15: **Quick Fuel Stop**]

Around the corner to the Somali run shop. He has everything we need and more. Makes me smiles as none of the locals has any shoes but he can sell me laces for my boots. Great guy and full of the joys. Coke and a chat about the world with him. Bit of an entrepreneur for these parts.

The road out of town found us staring at the APC and the Russian T-64 tank. Painted red lead these weren't abandoned but what they were doing there I don't know. They looked serviceable to me. Got more attention as I paid attention to the tank. He pointed out the whereabouts of the police station but I'm not going there. Maybe we should move on. It's not for me to judge.

Struggle for the next bit as the road has been used by all sorts to service this town and the sand is back. It's never far away really!

Not before long we come across some sort of clearing and a track that is cut back towards the railway line. It didn't take long to figure out it was a small cemetery. Back down the track to the railway line. I'm not keen in hanging around any cemetery.

No mines here, this track is freshly scraped out. There's a tree that has all it's surrounding grass flattened. Perfect! Your true wild camping spots in Angola. They don't come along too often. So sometimes you just got to take them. Noodles and another gift from Africa. Sunset… What a life!

[Video No. 16: **Sunset**]

The end of the track wasn't far. Another 40 km of riding the rails. The road, trail or track that we were meant to be following has disappeared. Not on the satnav as it was showing us following the correct route. Mmm… Tracks for Africa maybe not what it was cracked up to be. One of the few times we paid for the GPS maps and don't think we'll be doing it again. We thought it was smarter seeing we were going off the beaten track. Maybe they've not been here either!

More of the good stuff as we bump into an army patrol on the road. Erm! train track. Really must be the route of choice. Don't know who's more surprised. Us for meeting them whilst patrolling the track or them for having to step out the track to let us through... Bom-D and a wave, all was cool. We're no threat!

[Video No. 17: **Take a Look up The Railtrack**]

The tracks turned north and it was time for us to find the road. Easier said than done!

Water top up from the police checkpoint. They were cool even tried to sell us some Gasolina. Through a maze of forrest logging tracks. Bugga the softest sand yet. Real slow progress but we find the one we want. It's to take us to the main NJimbe road. It does but not before we ride through the sandpit once more. Another 40km of hell.

I did mention JackSparrow doesn't like the soft stuff. Didn't I? Things had been better after the fork oil change back in Luanda but we were still not getting on with the real soft stuff, no one can.

After some nifty riding the china line we popped out the other side. Wow! a new ribbon of the black stuff. Smooth, well smooth.

Short lived I'm afraid as that disappeared all too soon. The tar followed more of a north south route, heading for the now preferred crossing of Chavuma.

Village life was creeping up on us once more. The last village before the tricky section Justine the mechanic had warned us about a few days earlier. There's a crowd at the side of the road. Heidi does her Spanglish come Portuguess thing. The soba here couldn't have been any more different from the last.

So welcoming

Sit sit. You need a wash! Statement not a question. Water arrives and Heidi was handed the soap. Don't know what he was trying to say. Yeah we do. We were filthy. Wash in a bucket, as we have a crowd to entertain. Hey I do my best with the kids. The little ones being pushed to the front as I clown around. Soap in my eyes walking around like

Frankenstein. Whoops of laughter and giggles. Taking off my boots, one is stuck and I try to encourage them to help finally flopping backwards as it flies off. More giggles. I'm a star and didn't even know it. Just never found my audience before…Three and four year old Angolan kids that have never seen a white man…

Heidi's turn as she takes all their picture and shows them round. Funtime.

Need a lie down after that one. Sunset and noodles

Then another hard day ahead, of that I was sure, but there's always time for a quick cuppa and our morning goodbyes. Gifty for the soba and another photo session. Beautiful People. We're loving Angola again.

The road as it was did continue for a bit but not for long. The junction for Cazombe. We're taking the road less travelled though. The old road.

Bugga, hell is just around the corner I feel.

The sand started from the off, and there was no let up. Drenched in sweat before I knew it. This is as bad as I can cope with. Not really coping but there's nothing else to do.

Bog down and kick down into 1st gear. Spinning the rear and pushing with my feet till it gripped again. The process never changed and never halted. Over and over again. No Chinese scooter track to follow here. In fact there was only one set of tracks, a truck I thought. Just keep going. Stopping and starting every few meters. Bog down and kick down into 1st. Spinning the rear and pushing with my feet till it grips again.

What I nightmare!

There's a truck up ahead. Bugga it's been abandoned. Stuck in the mud of the rainy season, and not the sand of today. We ride around and carry on. Bog down and kick down into 1st. Spinning the rear and pushing with my feet till it grips again. Just not fun anymore.

Heidi has a moment in front of me. Not a big bike off but she bangs her shins of the foot pegs. Tears but so would anyone. Sit down for a minute.

Do you think we can make it? Wow if Heidi has her doubts then its tuff. She's more adventurous than any women I've ever met.

Sure just keep plugging away I tell her. But by now I'm having serious doubts myself. Work harder! Work harder!

Bog down and kick down into 1st. Spinning the rear and pushing with my feet till it grips again. Oops that's not spinning anymore. The clutch is slipping. Serious doubts now.

You're kidding not another checkpoint. Can't be, not out here. But sure enough. He invites us to sit in his lappa. Shade from the sun, not on his knee. We've been on the road 6 hours and only 35km and another 32km to the next village and the turn in the track. According to Justine it does get better. I'm just hoping it's from there. Jimmy's foot beginning to Struggle with the rigours of the trail.

A cuppa with the police as they play some version of drafts with bottle tops. An invite to stay in their compound for the night. Hey, the bike is not playing the game so we may as well stay. A welcome rest that's for sure.

They were cool. They ask about my tattoos and that in turn changes to them showing of pictures and telling me of their families. Get past the uniform and they're actually human. A bit unfair as they really were cool guys.

I took the chance to ask them about the truck back down the track. Raised eyebrows and a smile. Apparently it happened some six months back at the start of the rainy season and nothings been down the track since. I really can believe that one.

Push for the Frontera!

Up in the morning and the SatNav has changed time zones that's how close we are to the DRC border. We've been hand railing it most of yesterday and now all the way to Njimbe Frontera.

The track did get a bit better just as the police and Justin had explained. Jack Sparrows clutch did play the game what with my adjustments and an overnight cool down. It wasn't as bad as yesterday but he still needed encouragement to get out the starting blocks.

A combination of Feathering the clutch and creative riding. Well the good old china-line! We made better progress than the day before. Actually made us giggle in places, it was like Ski Sunday as we slalomed from side to side on the track searching for grip.

The village came and went with not much there at all. Can't believe it had a place on the map other than a turn in the track. Said hello and cheerio basically and round the corner yet another checkpoint. Waved on this time! Gunfire in the woods but they weren't bothered so I take it was their own, hunting I guess. We'll call it that and move on.

With no need for overtaking out here the track is still a single one. With more potholes and ruts than ever, but it's not the rainy season so we continue to slalom on. Weaving to-n-fro all morning continuing on into the afternoon. Awesome riding.

Did I tell you we loved Angola…

Village after village passed by with everyone waving as we went. The people just pleased to see you. A great feeling of friendliness. Something we've had from the offset at the border and I'm so glad it lasted right through to the other side as there is not many kilometres left.

The municipal village/town of Caiando. Left to the DRC and right to Zambia. It doesn't get much clearer than that. More wine bottles sitting on an oil drum so a quick fuel stop and yet another police checkpoint. But there is no hassle here. Friendly chat and some pictures. Glucose biscuits and a Coke out of the little shop. Hey! they didn't sell much else.

There was a growing number of dodgy phallic looking Termite mounds along the washed out road. To be honest they were massive and more than I can every remember seeing. Where did they all come from? More dried up riverbeds and yeah before you know it we're there.

Njimbe

Would you like processed tonight so to sleep in Zambia? Eh no, not really. The prospect of a late afternoon round of border control wasn't that appealing. We have one more day left on our visa so its an easy decision and one that needs no discussion.

Then you can stay the night here with us.

Good people, good chat. I guess they don't get many tourist out here. We were shown to the shower block. Females on the left of the bridge and males on the right. Its ok there is no crocodile in the river. We hadn't had a proper wash for a while so right in there. I had the gents to myself for a while until one of the locals came down. Not sure what he thought of the naked white dude covered in soap in his River... Bowatadi...

Processed the following morning, a strange affair getting searched on the way out and a thorough check of our particulars. To me a true sense of how much tourist traffic they get. Probably none. They were only doing their job and professionally done too.

Loving Angola...

After Angola we're Zambia bound. It's got stiff competition to beat in the friendly stakes...

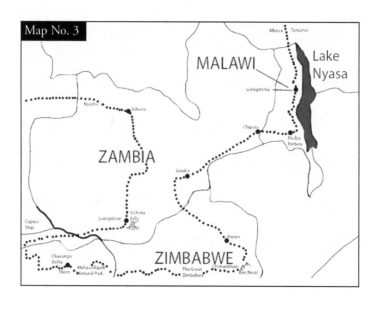

12
Tall order

It's a tall order for anyone to match the fantastic time we had in Angola.

Across the bridge into the land of the giant termite mounds. Don't know why but there just seems to be hundreds of them. Maybe more if I'm honest. Strange looking things but as we travel along the road there's mud brick workings next to the termite mounds. Ingenious really. Not sure but the mud bricks made from the mound must be quality compared to those made at the side of the river. I didn't stop to ask but it makes sense inside my head. The termite mounds are like concrete. Why else would you?

The Source of the Zambezi. We had thought that we would follow the river to Livingstone but the carbon tax mission we found ourselves on makes a difference. We were heading to Solwezi to pay it. There wasn't a customs officer at the border for whatever reason. Bunking off me thinks but we find ourselves travelling to town to pay it. What a joke!

Zambia wasn't that bad but the 1st stage of our 500km detour to pay the carbon tax (yeah carbon tax) was too much. It took its toll on us and we got a room in town for the night. The only downside being the spiders in the bathroom. Yeah another one to add to my chores list… Pest Control…

A slow lazy morning and our thoughts turn of going back to the supermarket for more supplies. Mmm… BigBed for a change. There's a Vidal Sassoon moment and a flutter of eyelashes "if you loved me" and I was heading to Shop-rite on my own as the Ngjinja Queen had her coffee and a lazy morning in bed.

Ended up staying another night and changed our plan of attack. A line shot down the middle!

[Video No. 18: **Zambia**]

We felt too tired to enjoy Zambia. The smile just wasn't there. No fuzzy feeling inside.

Looking back at the video when we arrived at Livingstone said different but it was still not Angola. Corrupt coppers at the border. Bent traffic officials at the road works and The Tourist Prices for all the little ferries took the edge off things. Hey! this is Africa I suppose.

Livingstone wasn't that good to be honest. The falls were great. Full of water and a refreshing experience but we just didn't gel with town. Road weary I guess. I was tired and Heidi had been here before. Got myself the worst haircut on the planet. Shit, I explained it well enough. Or so I thought! Ye, ye I understand then he done what the fuck he wanted. No tip for you my son. Listen to what your customer wants. A lesson for me for the future...

Tale From The Riverbank

Just had to get out of town and head for Botswana. Via Namibia and the Caprivi Strip.

Cross the border and find a campsite.

Sitting on the banks of the Zambezi we had originally said one night but hey! we couldn't leave.

It took us a week. We did nothing but chill, read, karate and the odd run on the bike to Shop-rite for provisions.

Jimmy's foot was heeling, more than that I really was getting back some mobility. It still hurt. Hurt like hell at times but I was more frightened about not using it. Scar tissue taking a hold... The road to recovery may not have been that easy. Sitting at home with me foot up might have been the smart move. But those few months crossing

Kaokoland, Angola and down through Zambia I wouldn't have changed for anything… What a Ride…

[Video No. 19: **Karate Kombo**]

We sat roasting nuts on the river bank of an evening watching the Hippos swim by. Calls from the Ibis ringing in our ears. Ha-De-Da … Ha-De-Da … Ha-De-Da. There was a few cold beers and the odd glass of wine to ease our suffering.

But never felt so relaxed in a long time and by the end of the week we felt truly refreshed. Heaven… Well we'd been talking on and off about where we're gonna live when this crazy road trip ends. Wherever home is gonna be that is. It could have been so easy to stay right here… Wonderful place…

The road goes on and with so much still to see that you can't sit still for ever, even if the place seemed perfect. Paradise on the banks of The Zambezi….

Along the Caprivi Strip and another camp by the river. Not the Zambezi but just as cool as there's a Crash of Hippos in the pool right next to us. We had been impersonating them all week and here they were, up close as you like… Just makes us laugh…

Cool photos and a training session in the morning. What a site. Almost convinced I seen my 1st elephant but can't be sure. He was running away from me. Maybe just wishful thinking.

But off once more. Camp before the border and hopefully some elephants along the way. There is enough of his calling cards by the roadside and I'm not imagining that.

Camp on the river once more. A serenade by the hippos and a big smile. Just can't stop laughing when we hear them. We have a giggle and drift off to dreamland.

Off down the track and across the national park boundaries. A dusty road but there is potential… Still living in hope…

Bugga me there he is. A Big Bull Elephant! Trashing the trees as he goes. A cool moment, for that was all there was as he goes on his way. My first Elephant in Africa. I'm not sure if it was what I expected. To excited to take it all in. It just happened to quickly but I'm smiling. A day full off wildlife to be fair, but that moment just special.

Border day once more and the easiest yet. Slick and off down the road. Got a few miles to go before Maun and our rendezvous with our DHL life support package. Remember the clutch thingy? JackSparrow still whining as I go.

A Peaceful night in the bush as Botswana makes it easy. Serenaded by the rush the Quelea bird on the wind. Ah the late evening flurry of the flyby before roosting for the night. Thousands of them floating and rolling on the evening breeze. Zzzz…

In the morning we bumped into Philipe. An American cyclist tapping it out on his way to CapeTown. I introduced myself without stopping. Chatting at his cycle pace for a while before waving goodbye. Heidi caught up and asked why I didn't stop. I will do in a mo.

2–3 kms later I stopped and flashed the stove. Tea and Dunkers were waiting before he arrived.

High-Jacked him from the sides of the road to join us. He's on a break from the Peace Crop working in Malawi. Great chat on all things teaching for the Peace-Crop at grass routes there. Big Smiles form him and I'm sure we brightened up his day. Made me smile too…

13

Monkey business

Maun and the wonders of DHL. Well a holiday weekend and a few days delay. But more chilling on a campsite on the edge of the delta. Met a few new friends in Gui, Gion, Shane and his father Greg. Great group all doing their own thing.

Sitting still gave us time for that trip into the delta proper. On or in a Mokoro. Dug-out canoe with our guide TT.

More money than we would normally splash out but well worth it. Never seen so much wildlife. And someone to explain that little bit more. More birds than I can remember. Things that would migrate from the UK. Birds that were used to wintering in the wet lands of south east England. Make me wonder.

Late afternoon and a shot of polling on the Mokoro for us. It looks easier than it really is. But we didn't fall in.

Off to the hippo pool, you never know your luck. It's a slow moving pace that allows you to suck it all in. Quiet and stealth like, we reach the Hippo pool.

There was a pair mating when we turned up. I say pair but the female was out of sight. Just glad she could hold her breath for as long as she could... The big fella had some stamina...

Bugga! seen a lot more than the heads and ears we were used too. Yawns and smiles all round. A real Crash of 8 Adults and a young one all in the same pool. We could have stayed forever. Laughing at their calls but darkness is falling and with the big guys calling card all around our campsite we wanted to be back before dark.

Chill out evening with a simple meal of veggie noodles, tuna and campfire bread. Washed down with a plastic cup of the red stuff. Hey it was my birthday after all... No cake but there's something about cooking your bread on the open fire... We were Happy.

More noises throughout the night but they all gave a little something to the experience.

Up early for a walking safari. Vervet monkeys and birds galore. An explanation of the Go-Away-Bird from TT. A Grey Lourie with a screech of a call. An early warning siren for all wildlife around of imminent and expected danger. Could do with one of those...

Then everyone stopped almost together. A big bull elephant shaking nuts from a tree no more than 50m away. Video camera and whispers. Along with a tap on the shoulder to retreat to safety. A bit carried away with the filming me!

Zebra, antelope, giraffe and more video footage than I've taken in months. Magic. Just Magic!

A slow walk back to camp with the images of our walk to make our minds go into overdrive. There's an elephant skeleton to explain and examine. No foul play we're assured but the tusks are missing. Apparently when the elephant ware out the last set their teeth they're very vulnerable. Can't eat and slowly die. Somber moment. The highs and lows of Mother Nature.

But back to earth with a bump as the campsite's looking a rather whitish kinda grey...

The vervet monkey earlier in the morning? He's came a calling when we were out.

[Video No. 20: **Monkey Business**]

Little Darling!

Trashed the tent here and there before finding the zip to let himself in. Mmm... last night's flour for bread was everywhere. Nothing escaped. Oh he's been all excited and shit all over my jacket too...

Getting harder to love these little beggars.

Nothing else to do but clean up and pack up. Head for camp.

[Video No. 21: **Okavango Delta**]

It took most of the afternoon to clean and repair the tent but on the bright side DHL had delivered and no customs charge. Happy Days!

The evening was spent with Shane and his dad, Aussies full of life and good company. There was a group of kayakers who had just finished a week's long journey through the delta. Had particular fun or mischief teasing them and their opinion of women explorers. Their views on Livingstone and the likes. All good fun but the Honey Liquor that Greg brought to the table was pure evil in liquid form.

Off to bed but not for long as the evil Honey burned the lining of my stomach. Bugga my first real hangover in Africa. Not Good!

I had left my monkey shit jacket outside for laundry. Only to find the camp dog peeing on it as I made my dash to the toilet. It doesn't rain but it pours, eh!!!

Lost a day out of my life. Hell in a Heatwave!:-(

The next few days were more productive. Changed my clutch and serviced the bikes. Astounded to find a chameleon siting under Heidis fuel tank. He must have been on the ride into town and back at least, maybe more. Put him in the tree and carried on. Nice distraction for a few moments. Knock a couple of links out the chain and see if I can delay changing my new chain and sprocket set. See if they'll last the journey across the Makgadikgadi.

Test run and a big smile. All is good with the world again. The Okavango has been good to us.

Crossing The Makgadikgadi Salt Pans

High on our list, we were both looking forward to this. Not as easy to get access on the bikes but hey! just give it a go. Head to Mopipi and camp at the roadside (Welcome J&H), nice welcome but I'll be surprised if the sign is for us.

Up and head off down the track heading for Chapmans Baobab. Ran into the veterinary fence first though. Heidi spoke nicely to the gate keeper and he let us through. Told us to follow the fence for 30km and ask the next gatekeeper to let us through. So we did.

Awesome ride as we passed over and skirted the little pans. But the gate came on us quickly.

The gate keeper was cool about it all. Matta, Much Matta. As he did tell us that it's privately leased (not owned) land on the other side. And if the warden from Jacks Camp on the other side gives us trouble don't be scared.

He didn't work for him. He worked for the government and didn't mind opening the gate.

Good, we didn't mind either.

He did however tell us that the Baobab might have fallen down some three months back but he wasn't sure. It's been a long time since he had visited and he was only telling us what he was told by other travellers that had come this way.

Off we went and enjoyed the ride. Well cool! More than that a truly wondrous place. One monster of a tree but he was right it lay in half a dozen pieces.

A sizeable billboard proclaiming this 500 year old tree as a national monument.

There's a reason that trees just don't grow all the way to the moon. A victim of its own success. Shame as it must have been massively impressive in its day...

Move on a little and into the bush. We weren't paying the exorbitant camping fee at the Jacks Camp. Incredible! No one can pay that kind of money, can they? Thousands of Dollars, what's that about?

Anyway a goodnight with not too much howling and off to Kubu Island in the morning. Still a tuff trail in front of us but we were looking forward to the big pans proper. When it came there was no disappointment. Amazing. Yip, some of it was just soft sand but the hard packed trails were immense. What a ride! Where the horizon line and the pans meet the sky, was only a thin grey line. Not much to tell them apart. A few desert zebra in the distance, oh and that strangest bird of all the ostrich. We played around for a bit making sure we got the photos we wanted before checking out Kubu Island.

[Video No. 22: **Kubu Island**]

What a place. Occupied by man for eternity it seemed and Fortified by the Great Zimbabwean Empire but there's always disappointment around the corner. The dreadful scars left by the BBC Top Gear Team driving across the Pans are still visible.

Ah the finger print of man!!! Scars across the Moon-scape that's in front of us… Mmm… But we enjoyed roaming around the island. A large tortoise shell shaped mass encrusted to the salt-bed. Pebble-dashed on all sides with Baobab trees like some sort of porcupined freak of nature. An amazing place to drift off into a daydream of what life could have been like when it really was a water locked island of old. Wonderful place to have a lazy afternoon.

Just can't bring ourselves to pay the camping fees, so off to the bush once more. All be it we had to get off the pans first. There's not that far to go. Watching the sun go down from our shore line, you really can't argue with the beauty that is The Makgadikgadi…

Francis Town here we come

Nice campsite and a resupply. Not to mention the shopping list. New tools for Jimmy but not all that had went missing in Kaokoland. Didn't close the tool-tube properly and they jumped ship in the desert. A new laptop for the crazy one. Hey! her MacBook had been on the blink since spilling water on it in Windhoek. It's not been the happiest of times for our Gadgets, but it's good to keep up to date with your diary. Essential even! Research on your phones not always easy either. Sometimes you just got to bite the bullet. Needs must and all that.

Thoughts of Zimbabwe

The lady on the campsite gave us good info about Zimbabwe as there had been unrest in the capital Harare. Pastor Jack organising stay aways. The corruption with the police had just got too much for the taxi drivers too so they were protesting. She was a wealth of info due to her daughter living there. But she never once told us not to go. So off we went.

14

The Great Zimbabwe

So We Did!:-)

Border wasn't that bad. In fact the immigrations guys couldn't do enough for us. Not sure if we paid all the right insurances and road taxes but we were let loose on the streets after a hearty laughing football fanatic at the customs gate. I've got into the habit of asking all Africans about football. It usually consist of talking Chelsea or Man Utd but they always ask me too. He took to hysterics when I mentioned the Famous Glasgow Rangers. Even he had heard of the how the mighty had crashed after the Tax-mans Affair.

More police check points than anywhere but they didn't stop us. I presumed they had been told to back off after the protest only a few days before.

We had picked up a lone biker from South Africa. Danny. Not quite how you say it in Africans but he didn't mind too much. Great chat about travel in general. He was eager to listen to our stories and ask even more questions. A man with itchy feet me thinks.

Up and a trip to Motopos National Park. We were looking forward to Worlds View but we got stopped in our tracks at the gate. No Motorbikes! We can hire you a bicycle though. Mmm... Doesn't make sense... Their rules I suppose and typical for Africa no one can explain why or take any decisions. To make matters worse a ladies running club trotted out the park gate. They asked us our story and without stopping for breath told us to follow them into town. They were going to lend us their car.

Awesome only knew them from the car park. Nice place this.

Along the road to Bulawayo my luck ran out and the coppers stopped me.

License.

No Lights. Fine!

Ur having a laugh. I'll turn them on.

No! Fine!…

FuckWit!

What a way to police a country.

I'm not giving them any money. I explained.

That's when Heidi and Danny stepped in. Offering to help but I wished they hadn't. Offer them nothing was all that was going through my mind. No help, no offers of any kind. Twats everyone of them.

The Sergeant did come over after his minion had waved his arms around for a bit. We never had our documents with us. More trouble but Heidi did sweet talk him into letting us bring them to the check point the following day.

Doesn't matter how you dress it up, they're nothing but thieves and I'm entitled to my opinion. Even if I'm not, it won't change what I think of them. Some people defend how they are far too much. That they don't get paid enough or at all, doesn't give them the right to exploit their fellow man. I'm just a tourist and get pissed off with it. Just can't imagine how I'd feel if I was a taxi driver and it happened on a daily basis. Bastards!

Motopos was cool but not worth the money or the days efforts to be honest but I can understand why Cecil Rhodes liked the place so much.

Up the next day leaving Danny to go on his own journey north to Vic Falls. We were heading east to The Great Zimbabwe Ruins. We had an appointment with the twats from the day before. It all went better than I thought. Showed him our paperwork, hell, after all that he had never seen a Carnet de Passage before and just handed it straight back. Never even finished my explanation of what it was and how it works.

Mmm... Move on.

A night in the bush as the ruins were too far for one days ride but the street venders cheered me up along the way. The good people of Zimbabwe didn't deserve a police force like they've got. Chit-chat with the locals always brings a smile to me face. The same questions really but there only curious about your journey and pretty pleased you came to see their country. All good.

Into the ruins the following day. Ah the Vervet. Not pitching my tent or leaving my gear unattended. Left it all in the reception. Changed and off to clamber around the ruins.

This place really doesn't get enough recognition. Built so long ago before proper tools it's just amazing. The ingenuity of man. More amazing is its still pretty much intact. You can't fail to be impressed. The museum was cool. Told its story and we were left alone to explore the site. Sat on the highest of perches in the hill complex trying to imagine who had sat here before me. Imagination runs wild as I sit there. Not sure if the Queen of Sheba sat here eating her cheese & Mr Balls chutney sandwich though.

We spent the rest of the day trawling the outer sites. Wondrous.

Truly Wondrous. Lost for superlatives. This place really caught my imagination. Just a pity my writing skills are not up to scratch.

Morning Blossom! Tea? If you loved me, with those pleading eyes of hers. Jump Up and out tent to make the morning tea. Mmm... tent surrounded by The Vervet Beasties. Time to introduce them to Tool-In-A-Can.

I had this idea for a while. If I keep my can of bike lube close to the tent door I could jump out and flash the lighter and spray. An instant Flamethrower!:-)

One quick blast would frighten away most beasts and then I could set about starting a campfire. Even the old Bushmen swore by the campfire for security. Most times having two of them and sleeping In-between.

But today the monkey pests where just getting the short blast to send them on their way. It didn't take much. 1-2-3 short blast was enough to send the 40 or so of them on their way... Little Beggars would steel anything and a whole lot more if you let them. Not sure it's the right thing to do but hey! we have a history. Shysters!

A cool twisty road around Kyle Dam was today's treat. Some proper engineering to build this but a few hundred meters on we're back to the Rondavels. Prehistoric the countryside a real throwback in time but a peaceful bliss about it too.

A couple of easy bush camps and we were approaching Chimanimani where we are gonna stop for a few days.

As the road climbed it was more like home than Africa. Pine Forest and plantations. Ok, maybe not bananas back home but you get my drift about the pine trees. Definitely not local to Africa. Colder and colder as we climbed, light fading and the mist swirling around us we really could be back home. Well almost...

YumYum

One night in Heaven we said. Heaven lodge and campsite that is! We had a room for a change, for 2 nights! Not like us but Heidi was cold I was too if I'm honest. Then we spent the rest of the week hiking in the Chimanimani National Park.

Had to pay the tourist tax as usual which was beginning to grip me. So different to home where we have the freedom to roam. Don't realise how lucky we are.

It wasn't that extortionate but it gripped none the less.

Let it slide and enjoyed the hiking. Heading for our mountain hut...

The park ranger at base camp had explained where the key for the storeroom was and we could get all sorts inside even leave our kit there while we went off exploring.

Late afternoon and off to Skeleton Pass. An old smugglers route to and from Mozambique. Sneaked across the border for 20m but more to get a better camera angle. Good shots. Peace and quiet for a bit.

A chat with the park rangers on the way down. More like army to be honest. Standing patrol on the old route. Apparently to deter gold panning by the border folk. 15 day patrols then 2 weeks off. Hey! I could think of worse ways to make a living. Joked with him that I loved his office. Nice guys. Happy to chat me thinks.

A cool night in front of the log fire in our mountain hut. An old farm cottage me thinks. A proper stone build one. What a view, all the way to Ben Nevis. Not its local name but it was marked on our map as so.

Off early and heading up Mt Binga the highest of the parks peaks. We had all day so plenty time for pics and video of the climb blooming beautiful and I'll be surprised if I find anywhere in Africa more like Scotland. Truly Beautiful...

[Video No. 23: **Chimanimani YumYum**]

Back to heaven for a few nights rest. It was Saturday and they were gonna fire up the pizza oven. Not the best pizza I've ever had but hey this is Africa. Tasty!.

A night with the ex-pat community. Most of them born in Rhodesia to be honest, and all of them from the older generation. I think Heidi and me both realised it. There was a generation gap here. The younger ones had all gone abroad to study or just escape the madness that is Mugabe.

We can't judge but only listen, they're all hopeful that things are a changing.

The Road Less Travelled

Took the old road to Chatta and Mutare. Great ride and one that Heidi was willing to take to the front for a change. Yip, you guessed it. Bloody Dusty and no fun at the back. Good ride none the less.

[Video No. 24: **The Road Less Travelled**]

Rest day in town and a visit to the Mozambique Consulate. It only confirmed our fears. Not paying that kinda money for a transit visa and the prospects of a security convoy. We'll take the detour back to Zambia to get to Malawi. There's no ridged plan to stick to.

A day in the hills outside town, where we bumped into some locals. Local Rhodesians that is. Wonderful group of ladies out to visit a local flower nursery. Brought along their picnic and Alex's the Tai Chi instructor. Great chat and an invite to join in. What a cool day.

Karate is my thing but you got to have an open mind to all sorts.

In between sessions of Tia-Chi we would chat about all things Zimbabwe, Rhodesia and Southern Africa. It wasn't all serious though as we discussed everything from the second hand clothes market to the variety of birdlife Africa had to offer. We're no twitchers but we had made up names for what we had seen and heard along the way.

The Ha-De-Da or *ibis* – The Work-Harder-Bird or *Ring-Neck Dove* – The Squeaky wheel barrow bird – The internet Dial-up bird – The Go-away-Bird *Grey Lourie*. Some not needing any real explanation but Squeaky Wheel barrow? Just a play on its call or squawk. Makes us laugh. Hey! They sang a song to us of how your goats have gone and run away. A variation of the dove. Childish I know but when you've not got the answers for what you see and hear. Why not?

They recommended Seldom Seen Campsite, a twitchers paradise and that was that. Yip, you can camp or have the chalet. It wasn't furnished but the kitchen and bathroom functioned. Sat outside roasting monkey nuts of an evening. Lovin' Zimbabwe. Well most of it for it wasn't long before we would have to go...

It really was great to be away from the Taxi Madness that is, Lionel Messi – Safety First – Armageddon – Street Assassin. What are they thinking when they paint this on the side of their cabs?

You had to watch them all as they'd cut you up at the sniff of another fare. Bastards… Scourge of Africa…

Harare and what we said we would avoid but this was cool. A quick hit and run to the Apple Store with the MacBook. No joy but a great cup of coffee with the owner. More chat about Mugabe. Things are a changing or so it seems.

The road to the border…

No sooner out of town and yip, yet another police check point.

Fine $40. 10 dollars, 10 dollars, 10 dollars, 10 dollars as he walks around our bikes. To me it felt that Heidi had defended the Fuckwit copper when he wanted to fine me for not having my lights on. Seemed a different story when they were trying to fine her for no reflectors. Yeah reflectors.

Apparently on your car you need them back and front. White on the front, red on the back. In sticky tape fashion.

Well ours are only on the back and in hard plastic. $10 U.S. each reflector.

She went to town on him. I want to see it in writing, she demanded! He struggled to find it. Claimed that the bikes were first commercial vehicles then motorised cycles. It wasn't until Heidi pointed out the motorcycle section that she got any joy.

You could see him deflate as he knew he was onto a loser. No $40 for his back pocket. Return of the license and have a nice day.

I was glad to stay out of it as my indicator mount had broken and I'd not seen it happen till that moment. I'm sure that would have put the smile back on his face. Thief!:-(

Back on the road with a smile on her face Heidi feeling pleased with herself. You got to get up early in the morning to catch her out…

Too far to the border so another night in the bush. A smaller road through Charara safari area to Kariba?

Nice and twisty!

This reminds me of a topic on the Horizons Unlimited website.

Question:- Motorcyclist? Or Motorcycle Traveller?

Here's the answer... When you see the sign post Danger! Warning! Twisty roads for the next 5km! What's the first thing that comes into your head?

a) Check your mirrors, turn on your Helmet Cam and knock it down 2 gears. Answer – You're a Biker!

b) All other options? Do I need to say more? Motorcycle Traveller!

Personally I knocked it down 2 gears. I can check the helmet cam footage at the next campsite... No sense in wasting a good set of twisties...

Warthogs BushCamp Kariba. It's not every day you ride into town and there's a family of stripey donkeys on the road. Eh, ok Zebra that would be. Another first. It's usually the donkeys you're taking avoiding action for but this time it was the stripey version. Carry on to the bushcamp and find a tent space. Mmm... elephants footprints are you sure?

Bugga it was. Hey! I'm sure it will be ok.

Sure enough not 20 mins later the tent was up and a cuppa on the go. Sat down and leaned back to enjoy my surroundings. Eh, Heidi is that what I think it is? Yes! Not 1 but 3 Elephants trashing the trees not 100m from where we sat. Just sat and stared for the next half hour almost forgetting my tea. Great day!

Pity about the night time hours though. Our hippo serenade was spoilt by the group of Irish Backpackers. Mmm... the Cosmopolitan Nation...

Over the border and heading for Lusaka. Easy enough and managed to pass on one of the old $100 US dollar bills. Nice money changer for a change. Not sure he was that happy though.

Hey! it still works in Zimbabwe I'm sure he'll pass it on...

15
ZimZam

Can't say I really enjoy the big city but we thought it was the thing to do. The one last chance to purchase the things that are a missing. But not really.

The bike shop was a disappointment. I only managed to pick up a spare set of spark plugs. No tyre levers to be had. Pretty much all that was left on my list to replace but we still had 2 between us.

Chill for a day and a visit to the cinema with pizza and a cold one. Very civilised.

Got chatting to a kinda local lady at the wash station. She had moved to Bologna with her Italian husband some 12 years before and was back visiting. More questions about our journey and amazement that Heidi was on her own bike. She must be strong! She's that and a whole lot more…

There's a confession that sticks with me, about the Mzungu. All white people have money she used to think. It's the impression that all Africans have. But not after living in Europe for so long, her thoughts had changed.

You own nothing!

You only say you own that house and that car. All you do is pay the bank to have the privilege to say so!

I'm sure that's right of your everyday African working class but there is a middle class here too! Sections of the community which Ooze success. Mmm…

Out of town and head towards the border and Chipata. We had a message from Gui our Korean friend saying she was held up in a lodge there. It's as good as any place to head to.

Not in one day though. The 560km journey, far too much for the little bike in one day.

A couple of nights bush camp along the way but we were there early on the 3rd day. Time to really catch up with the chores and Gui along with her new friend Luka. An Italian cyclist who had himself got stuck at this lodge. He was a chief so he plied his trade there. The place was managed by another Italian couple so I could see how it was easy for him.

A well-chilled out place and yet again we stayed longer than we thought. A couple of nights turned into a week once more. Spent the nights chatting to the various travellers who passed through. A group of Tanzania bikers. A Dutch cyclist couple and various backpackers. But we did enjoy ourselves. Heidi could kickstart an idea for a novel she had. I trawled the bike shops and street markets for tyre levers. No joy but I had an idea, maybe one of the metal workers could fashion one out of the 22mm ring spanner I had picked up. I never used the open end and asked if he could grind an end to look like the tyre leaver I had. Nothing seemed to be a problem. Well if there is electricity that is. Come back at 15:00

Off to the Barbershop for round 2.00 in Zambia. I was determined not to get the same treatment as last time. YeYe, we can do a good job after I explained what I wanted and what happened before. You fuck it up and I'm not paying! You understand? Not quite what I was used to back home. A bit unconventional with his cutting techniques. I'm no expert but they refuse to use the scissors, insisting on the clippers instead but the end result was ok. So I parted with some cash and we parted as friends.

Can't believe Gui had sat through the whole ordeal. Well not exactly sat still, as she had popped up in the chair next to me taking the scissor that weren't in use to her fringe.

Gui made us laugh in so many ways. Bubbly, full of life and happy to speak to the locals. Well nearly always...

Probably one of the funniest things I'd witnessed in Africa. I was chatting to the local youths about football as usual when Gui came out of the chemist shop. "Hey China" was the cry. Never seen her ignore anyone before then as she lifts her head securing the strap on her helmet…

I'm not China!
You look like China!
You look like eer Nigerian, yeah Nigerian!
No I'm Zambian.
No! You sure? Maybe Congo them…

By this time I had clicked but he hadn't.

He almost lost the plot. *My mother, My father all Zambian* as he beats his chest with his fist. He just can't see what she's up to.

Look mate all Asians are not the same. She's not China I whispered.

Never seen an African shrink back into themselves so quickly. So that line of all black dudes look the same does work both ways… makes me smile…

He does laugh…

But the Hey China thing was beginning to grip Gui. It's true. Africans have probably only ever seen Chinese construction workers or shop keepers. Maybe they knew of Japan but not any other Asian country. To be honest If anyone was ever gonna tame Africa it was probably gonna be the Chinese. They have a huge influence all over Africa.

Back to pick up my newly formed tyre lever. It was better than I expected. Not the light weight high quality finish of the motion pro tyre leaver I had lost but as good as it gets for these parts and a fraction of the price. He was happy with his $6 and me too. Gave a further buck to Tom for his fixer organiser role in this. Sorry just couldn't get my tongue around his African name but he did have a giggle at me trying. Along with everyone else within earshot, hey Mzungu business is good business and a laugh at him to.

After a week of the lodge it was time to go. There was a general election the day after and we were all eager to avoid it. Zambia is a very stable country but we're not that keen to push my luck.

A chat with the money changers to get some dollars US for the up and coming borders. They rallied around and came up with $300. Changed our Zambian for Malawi Qwacha with some trouble. It's never easy when you're dealing with thousands. Chancers, but I'm sure we're good.

Back to the ATM for more cash and do the deal. If it wasn't so painful it would be impressive. I thought I was watching and Heidi normally sharp but they still done us.

We should have got up earlier that morning.

The $300 was flashed in front of Heidi and she handed over the 33,000 but only $200 came over. To many hands in this deal and the fuckwit doing the counting has now changed the rate. In the confusion he slipped 300 behind his back to his mate and we never even saw it. By the time the argument stops and we have back our Qwacha it's all to late. I been had says Heidi. Fuck this as I get off my bike. Wanted turn the little fucker upside down as he pleads his innocence. He even offers to go to the police with me as he turns out his pocket. Bastard! I wanted to hit the twat there and then before I came to my senses. Supermarket car park with no real escape route.

Bastard!

You're nothing but a fucking thief! Thieves always get what's coming to them. Believe me you'll get yours! On my bike and go $30 short.

Not the biggest loss in the world but it was the way it was done. Fuck! I can't believe I'm so stupid. I know Heidi felt worse as she was meant to be the wise one. Told her to forget it and move on. It will eat at you if you don't.

Wise words but ones I couldn't follow myself as I revved my bike harder and harder down the road constantly cursing myself for letting Fuckwit off with it...

Thankfully an easy border crossing and catch up with Gui. We rode to the same campsite in Lilongwe together.

What a shit day. Lost our laptop power lead....... And the Bastard money changer. What next?

Just Another Day

A night in the local Korean restaurant. Mmm... I've heard all the stories and opted for the vegetarian option. No doggy for me!:-) but when I handed over the money to Heidi to pay it was 10,000 Qwacha short. I couldn't bare to recount the money thinking we had been stung twice by that little bastard... A restless night...

Up early with the world challenge group making all the noise. Took a bit of restraint not to go over and smash the boombox. I'd only be taking out my frustration from the day before on them. Not our favourite campsite. Chill pill required... Maybe just the paracetamol.

Heidi ran off into town in search of a new laptop power cable. Success after shop No.11 Not sure I'd have persisted that long.

16

Pottering around

Time to get out of town...

Dedza Pottery was our destination.

Something we had read about in the guide book. Good campsite and a chance to go hiking. It was just what we needed. A Fantastic place. If we had a house I'd have bought our dinner set there and then. Had it all picked out between us but we haven't bought a house yet. Maybe online later.

Up in the mountains means you have to come down. A magic set of twisties for the road to lake Malawi. The memory of being stung by the money changer almost eradicated from my mind.

Turned into Mua. The local mission and craft centre. It was mobbed. Can't leave the bikes with all their gear so I sent Heidi into have a look see. I gave the local kids my 1st Nunchucka Street Performance. Hey it distracted them from interfering with the bikes. If fact a local guy came over and asked for a shot. Said he used to play with them as a kid. He showed me a new trick so all was good. Kids seemed to like it to. I may do more of these.

A good run into Senga Bay and a chance meeting with Gui once more as she was going the other way down the lake to MacClear. Roadside gossip as she explains her plans with Luka had moved on somewhat to meeting up in Venice and travel to South America together. She's a bit of a romantic me thinks...

Busy in Senga Bay campsite but stayed anyway, thankfully the music was turned off at 10. Saturday night. How rock n roll are we. Not really had that many good nights sleep of late.

Moved on to Nkotakota and found something more peaceful. A chance to enjoy beach life for a bit. Heidi busy writing and a chance for me to catch up with stuff. Easy life for a few days, still customising her jeans. Just Lovin Malawi…

Market Days

Life goes on even while sitting still so it's always good whenever we go to market. Market days are what life is all about. Locals doing local things. Everything grown locally that's for sure. Well as locally as anyone can carry it! Almost everything grown cooked or made within walking distance of this happy gathering. That makes it sound a small gathering and very local, but you'd be surprised how far people are prepare to walk. Obviously there are plenty who'll deliver for a small fee and that all important supply of all things made in china.

A labyrinth of alleyways to-ing and fro-ing between wooden stalls and shacks. Some sharing tables and racks while others a mere wooden box to show off their wares.

It's a hustle, it's a bustle but it's life with all that it brings…

[Video No. 25: **Market Day**]

The Great Fish Warriors

I sit relaxing and catching up on my chores for the day. Can't fail to notice the kids on the beach. From dawn to dusk! It starts earlier, sometimes even before dawn. Talk about the early bird, they're there. You're not much use in your early years so you're tied to your mothers back and almost forgotten about. Taken everywhere but never included in what's going on. As soon as you're up and running you're put to good use. You're under the control of the older kids, brothers, sisters extended family. Here your job is to comb the beach first thing in the morning, in search of any booty the Great Lake will throw your way. Little fish washed ashore by the wind or strong under currents. Slightly bigger fish caught in little pools and a bit of general scavenging. Beach combers of the great lake.

They march up and down the beach with their metal bowls and plastic buckets full of what the lake provides. The bigger fish are skewered on bits of wire and carried as a badges of honor.

Later in the day it's more of the same with the slightly older kids doing their best to fish from the shore and scouring the pools. I sat transfixed to the happy hunter dance as one particular kid catches his prize.

Holding his fish high above his head, shaking his ass in the direction of his fellow hunter gatherers while boasting and bragging of how great he is!:-) A strange sight to behold. A little black kid in red underpants performing such a traditional ritual.

There is other pursuits. There's always time for a game of something. I watch them perform summersaults and back flips for each other and at quiet moments of training/practicing on the down low. Keeping their next performance a secret until the last minute.

The females arrive and its wash day. An array of clothes are washed and then stretched out on the sand. They sit around chatting and laughing. I can't help but think this is one of the more pleasurable of their many chores. The true backbone of the African family...

Sunset approaching and yet more beach combing and fishing the pools, the young marching behind but never far from the older ones. Not the Xbox generation of the western world but children going through a real apprenticeship of life... Meanwhile the older kids, well, the young men, progress to dugout canoes before being promoted the fully fledge night-time fishing boats.

In themselves they are impressive, a whole fleet of them. Maybe forty or fifty all in a line strung out across the horizon, bright white lights aglow acting like a strobe as they bob up and down. This is not done in the evening hour but throughout the night. Men more coordinated and trusted to bagging a serious catch before the daybreak procession back to shore where the day's proceedings starts all over again...

Lake Malawi, Mmm... what a Life...

Going North

Time for the road once more, refreshed and ready to go explore. We're heading north. Well, inland and heading for the hills but generally north.

Heading to the hills and hopefully some more hiking. Forest lodge sits half way between us and Nkata Bay, kinda! Seems like a good enough place to head for. Off the road a bit but it has caught our eye. A chance of hiking and whatever the forest lodge can offer, we'll take that any day. Some of the hiking Trails sound just like us...

A great ride rolling along the meandering ribbon of road. Not always tar but always rolling, meandering and a joy to ride. Nearly! The over used logging tracks that make their way to the lodge have turned to dust. Yip! the Crazy-one takes to the front once more. Seen this one before but I don't really mind.

A stunning lodge settled in a peaceful spot high up on the ridge looking down over the forest plantation. Great spot! There's plenty of choice to stretch our legs the following day.

The Fire-Watch look-Out Post

Up with the lark and Bob the Racist Ridgeback! I laughed when they said at the lodge he was racist but he certainly didn't like the locals working there. We woke to find him sitting outside our tent. A monster of a dog, even for a ridgeback. He just takes his security job seriously as he goes into one when the lodge staff make their way along the track to the lodge. Over zealous maybe but hey! I didn't employ him.

Some braving the brisk walk by, without looking. Some pushing a bicycle keeping it between them and this monster that's Bob, whilst others prepared to pay the toll fee with a treat. He's a happy puppy then… just made me laugh.

Up the hill along the forest trail skirting around the forester's village passing by the hillside lake. We could see the Look-Out post in the distance glimpses through the trees as we followed the printout given to us at the lodge. Just a sketch map but its good enough with the description by whoever walked this walk before us.

A great trail but the Look-Out Tower is on the high ground for obvious reasons. It's been here for many a year manned by dedicated plantation staff with a watchful eye. Ready to raise the alarm in case of fire. Early warning for what is the communities livelihood. The last stretch is a bit of a slog but worth it as you find out the reasons why it's there. What a view!

A brief chat with those who man the tower and an invite to see what they see. They see it all for miles around. That rolling Plantation in various states of cultivation. Some sparse, some growing, some just blowing in the breeze. Good job if you can get it.

Peace to eat our lunch on our happy hilltop.

Back to the lodge for an evening banter with the other guests. All Good!

Nkata Bay

The road takes us back towards the lake once more and Nkata Bay. Plenty of options for places to stay but we run straight into one as we take stock and a check of the map. We did have a name in mind but we were looking for somewhere to service the bikes once more. Time for another oil change and definitely time to change the chain and sprockets I've been carrying. I've had my money's worth out of these ones along the easy roads but on the forest tracks the chain had been slipping like a slippy thing. Here was good enough…

Run by locals this little place clung to the side of the cliff looking out over the bay. We pitched the tent as usual but the lofty little ledge barely big enough for the tent! it was different from the norm, well cool.

Town has virtually everything. Well, on a small scale but plenty going on. Even have the opportunity to treat my lady to a Tai Meal in the swankiest restaurant in town. WooHoo!:-)

Service day is becoming a well-rehearsed affair. Start up the Engine with then turn off the fuel tap, warming up the engines before draining the oil. Run the fuel out of the carburettors before removing the overland fuel tank. Never easy if it's full but I do try to predict the timing of the service to coincide with a lower fuel tank level.

Check the Valve Clearances are within tolerance. Turning the engine to read Top-dead centre always helps excess oil reach the now open drain plug. Clean, Inspect and replace if necessary the spark plug, the air filter and the oil filter. Yip! we carry them all and if spares are used then they're immediately added the shopping list for next time.

Then just move on with checking the rest of the bike. Checking everything for serviceability. It's not the first time that somethings just fallen off. We carry a complete selection of cap screws for all occasions. A few gaskets and "O-rings along with throttle and clutch cables. Not much else but you just can't carry it all. It's all become a well-rehearsed routine.

Before I know it, the days over but so is the servicing of both the bikes. Always a good feeling. But this time there a small weeping oil run from the Crazy-ones oil filter cover. Mmm… on inspection there's no 'O-ring? And I don't have a spare for this one. God only know where it went…

There's none to be had in town in any shape or form. I carry Duct Tape, Cable Ties, Fence Wire and a Leather Strap with hole punched in it for all occasions. Mmm… just cut one out of that. Ten minutes with the knife and its in there. Jobs a good'un. Not a perfect fit but when the leather absorbed the oil it all seems to close up and the leak stops. I'll remember this one… Happy Days…

Tyre Monkey

A quick visit to the cliff-top wood carvers cafe. Not exactly looking for gifts to take home. We can hardly carry what we've got, but the view is spectacular. The coffee isn't that bad either. While waiting on breakfast we did take time to look around his stall. Cool stuff really all hand carved in the community. Three legged table carved out of one piece of wood. Strange chairs with stranger tribal carvings but there's no room. There was even the strange board game we had seen at the lodge the night before, Bow… He tried to talk us into postage. DHL would you believe? Eh just bad tourists me thinks, but I was generally tempted.

Satisfied, we're leaving our lofty ledge and heading out of town. A day's short ride to The Mushroom Farm at Livingstonia. Yeah you heard me… The Mushroom farm… Easy road into town and Mizuzu Yamaha. Surprised me but if we could get a new "O"ring that would be cool.

The guys checked the entire stock of "O"rings as the Serow just wasn't on their list. No joy! Probably one of the few drawbacks of bringing the little bikes to Africa. The availability of spare parts but after changing a starter clutch early on I didn't think it would have been a tiny little piece off rubber that would be the problem. The leather is still holding in the oil and it really wasn't leaking. Just go with it. Shoprite for essentials and were off proper.

An easy days ride we thought. Uphill and down dale switchback heaven passing coal mines and rubber plantations as we go. Following flowing rivers and lake shore. Pretty cool. All too easy me thought as I look into my mirrors. An empty road behind which isn't too unusual. Not unusual for the Trick-cyclist to stop and take a picture of whatever really. We all see different thing as we go.

I stop and turn off my engine but no thump of the Serow engine from behind. Turn it around and go see what's happened. Oh she's taking the luggage off the bike.

No! The rear tyre is flat…

Been keeping an eye on the tyres for a while. We've not had many issues but this is the first puncture in Africa. It was bound to happen sooner rather than later. But it kinda goes out of your mind after a while.

Just need to get on with it. A whacking great piece of metal. Maybe a piece of wheel spoke, not ours thankfully but it was the size of a three inch nail. Straight through the tyre. Time to get out one of the spare tubes we'd been carrying.

[Video No. 26: **Tyre Monkey**]

It didn't take that long to be fair and not sure we really needed the practice at that particular moment in time but what are you gonna do? A quick turn around and back on the road. Maybe it's not gonna be as short a days ride as we thought.

With all the messing around in town and now this, we were gonna run out of daylight!

We can always camp at the side of the road if there is no one around. Just not sure that's gonna be the case. You only have to stop for the briefest of moments before you've got an audience.

Down towards the lakeside and the last stretch of the shore road before turning uphill towards Liningstonia and The Mushroom Farm. There's no chance of stopping anywhere. The roadway's a wash with people. It's like market day all along the road. Mmm…

With the light fading we take a look at each other? Up The Hill?

Now if it was a normal hill and a normal road it would be fine but this switchback dirt track in the dark was not heaven. Steeper than steep and not easy to follow as it climbed into the heavens. Not sure we could actually see the top in the dusk that was. Light was fading fast and we should just get on with it if were going.

It didn't take long before it really was dark. No street lights out here no stars yet and certainly no moon. This was earie!… This was everything they tell you not to do. A dirt road you don't know in the dark never mind the switchbacks the over the edge plunge down into hell. We'll take our time and if we can't see we'll just stop. Ok!

I have no idea how long it took to wind our way to the top. First gear, second gear at a push. Constantly stopping to check we were ok and managing to cope. I got into the swing of things and the Crazy-one was prepared to follow. Onward and upward checking the twists in the trail on my satnav. Trying not to get too fixated on the screen as the track was more important. We were making progress stopping to check the distance to the top. The kilometres ticked away and before we knew, it was very close.

There's a flash of lights from behind followed by that hard revving of an engine. Stop and there's silence… I ran back to find the bike on its side with that sweet stench of unleaded as fuel is running down the side of the bike.

No explanation as it's a mystery to the Crazy-one what happened but I knew we had to stop. According to the satnav the turn off to the campsite should be here.

How we missed it I don't know, or maybe I do but within 10mins we find the turn off for the next one up the track. This will do… Pitch the tent, Shower and check for bruises. Hey there's plenty of padding. Smiles and a beer as we laugh at ourselves for a trail we shouldn't have taken in the dark… Dreamland and see what the morrow brings.

The Mushroom Farm

Up with the lark and morning coffee with a view. Over the edge and a look at how far we had climbed the night before. Mmm… Stunning. The only drawback was there is nowhere to charge the keyboard players laptop. I'm not a writer but I can appreciate if you've got an idea, you should go with it. Heidi seems motivated to write and if this isn't the place we can move on. We can go in search of what we missed last night. The turn off for The Mushroom Farm.

One cool place to another. Not as refined but just as cool when looking over the edge of the cliff. In fact another lofty ledge to pitch our tent.

We opt for a tour of the coffee plantation as the laptop charges. We love coffee but I couldn't tell you what it looks like. Not even sure what the bush come tree looks like. We were about to be educated.

Only a short walk and you can see lots of small holdings clinging to the mountain side. We turn up the track to find our host and his kids tending their plot. Introductions and smiles all around. There's no real need for our guide as John our host has got a good grasp of English and takes time in telling his story. A hard working farmer that turns his hand to anything that grows but you can see his passion for coffee.

He sends his kids to pick the fruits for that's exactly what it's like. Grape like in size ranging from green to relish black in colour. There's a hand wound grinder which separates the seed from the fruit for it's the seed that's the good bit. The good ones sink into the bucket of water that catches the seeds. While the not so good float to the surface. The floaters are not for his coffee.

They are taken to the wash station to wash some more before being spread out on the drying tables. A process which can take up to two weeks. Once dry they look more white than black, something that doesn't occur until the roasting of the bean.

Back to his house for a cup. Just magic! Not the cup of Joe you can purchase at the service station and certainly not the overpriced skinny low fat latte with a shot of whatever. Just a good cup of coffee.

The chat in itself was priceless. An explanation of how he opted out of the local cooperative to sell straight to the Kenyan buyer which comes this way. More for him and his family. I hope this is what is meant when you read that **Fairtrade** Sticker on your Kenyan Roast Coffee…

Good coffee and good people…

Oot-n-a-boot sightseeing all things Liningstonia Mission Post. A Visit to the church and the Station Museum. Closed for lunch so step into the local lodge come cafe. Wonderful surprise with a wonderful people. They have rooms with a view. Mmm… how much? Before you know it we've made a deal to stay for a while. We'll be back tomorrow with all our kit...

Just at that, the Funny Korean chick we keep meeting passes us by once more. She's at the end of a 3 day hiking trail, new friends and guide in tow. Hello and a chin-wag. We ferry her and her kit to the Mushroom Farm. She can rest and get a bus from there she says. Always good to chat as she really makes us smile.

Gui stayed for a few days and so did we but she said her goodbyes once more promising to stay in touch the best we could. Fellow travellers it's what we do...

Move to the community lodge. It's what we want for a while. Heidi wants a few days to put some writing down on paper and me I don't mind. Wash and service all our kit. Try fixing the troublesome stove. There's always things to do and you don't always take time out to do them.

A chance text from Lizzy and James with the 4x4 truck we met in Namibia. They were on their way through. Well, not exactly but a run up the hill could be arranged. Beer, BBQ and good company, what more can you ask. A catch up on all things from home. Only the one night though, as they had plans of their own.

Livingstonia was all we expected and more. An unexpected chance to catch up with friends, well that was just a bonus... Loved it but we can't stay forever... A thank you to the ladies at the lodge for looking after us. Such a peaceful time.

Eh,no! Just before you leave you can have another puncture. Jacksparow this time. Just get on with it. Before your ride back down the hill.

Oh the hill! If I had seen this before I came up in the dark I'm not sure we would have taken it on... Maybe we would have just the same...

Korongo before hitting the border into Tanzania. Not much to see. It's big enough and has more than most towns of late but a means to an end. A cheap room, The Bank and a resupply, but that's enough for now

Tanzania

We're heading for Lake Tanganyika. It's a few days ride but in bite size chunks. Some road, some dirt trail and some of the unknown. Uphill and down dale passing through the tea and coffee plantations towards town. A night in Mbeya at the church mission.

Much more affluent and a real city with all that comes with it. Not that we're looking for it but its there. You know what I mean. Street life, cafes and bars a plenty. Spent the evening eating and chatting to the locals. All good.

Smaller towns and smaller villages but always enough. Cafes, shops, bars and good conversation to be had. There never seems to be any trouble in finding somewhere to stay. Guesthouses a plenty with a welcome smile. Just a cool couple of days. But the road does run out and we're on the dirt once more. It shouldn't be that far to the lake but the wobble of yet another puncture. No! But hey! Just get on with it… there's a routine forming here.

It's not that bad but there's a crowd of kids starting to form as I strip down the rear wheel and change the tube. Heidi takes out the camera and they all go running. It amuses us and a smile is always a good place to start. Our tyre pump is not working so we rely on one of the local kids to take us to someone who has. Success!

Gifty for the nice lady. They're all impressed that Heidi's out here riding her own bike. Something that's never going to happen for them. Bonn Route as it sounds to me, farewell as I feel like the pied piper riding out of town with a squabble of kids following behind.

We enjoyed the road, there was no tarmac but an endless stream of road works as we went. Bridge here, culvert there and excavations everywhere. Maybe this is why the satnav wouldn't route us this way. There just isn't a road really, but it's on its way.

Lake Tanganyika came all so soon. It might be late in the day but I just didn't know where the time had gone. The road probably! but wouldn't change it. I'll leave that to the Chinese.

Lodge Liemba

Down the steepest of hills towards the lodge. Wow! not looking forward to climbing back up that one already. Just so glad it was as good as it was. Beautiful guesthouses and chalets for sharing but we chose the old time styled safari tent on the beach. And what a beach. Converted Boathouse bar with a patio restaurant. What a place but where is everyone? Almost deserted as we're the only guests. I can live with that... for a while anyway, just didn't expect to spend as long. Just settled in when the news arrives that the Liemba is delayed... It often is. She has not even passed on her route south never mind the northern journey that we were hoping for. The guesthouse owner explains that the timetables a little flexible.

Sit back and enjoy what Kisanga and the lake have to offer. We spent our days enjoying the beach once more, but a trip into town was on the cards.

Kisanga is not much of a town, in size anyways. More of a staging area for what comes off and on the Liemba. It had enough. It kept us entertained anyway.

On the way into town we met the locals. Mothers with kids in-tow and on their backs, kids a plenty on their way to school, fishermen stretching out their nets for drying or repair. Lakeshore life in a different guise as there's plenty kids not at school but heading out in there dug-out canoes to do some fishing. A different lake, a different country but the same way of life really...

We met Pongo and his mates, a local lad drying himself on the shore. They'd all been swimming I suppose. He runs up and asks if he could get his picture taken with Heidi. Yeah it's ok. Heidi laughs at the size of his... trunks but we get a picture taken, Pongo standing in between us. He's giving me the stare. WTF? I just don't know what this is all about. More chat with Heidi rather than me. Another Facebook boyfriend me thinks but she's cool with it. He shows us around town, we buy him fish and rice for lunch. He was cool though, good chat of what's what around town. Not that much...

Nothing for it but to relax and enjoy the lake. So we did!:-) Ha-De-Da ... Ha-De-Da

Dinner on the lakeshore patio at sunset, it just doesn't get any better. Watching the local fishermen set about pushing off in search of their catch for the evening. It's not long before we're settled on our beachside bed mesmerised by the huge oil lamps out there floating on the water. It's not long before we've drifted off into dreamland. Beautiful place...

Map No. 4

17
Ah! The Liemba

We met Patrick and Rachel way back in CapeTown, friends of Heidi's really but a wonderful couple (I hope I can call them friends too). They told us of their journey down through Africa and their time on the Liemba. Fantastic stories.

I did remember the Michel Palin Pole to Pole thing, and it intrigued us both. Something we kept on the back burner for traveling north.

Not cheap, but She was worth every penny and the wait! But hey! that's one of her charms. The timetable is pretty fluid shall we say. We were 2 days early and she was 3 days late. Like the best of leading ladies she kept everyone waiting just to keep up that mystique.

Ok, maybe the mystique bit passed us by as we camped on the quayside, but this is Africa!

[Video No. 27: **Ah! The Liemba *All Aboard***]

Bikes up on Deck

Everyone who's getting off! Get off!

It didn't take long and we were called forward. The harbour master talking shit to me once more. You need to pay, you need to pay.

For what? I gave you money last night for embarkation.

The Bike, the bike.

The crew are doing the lifting not your men.

And at that it was left to me to sort them out as they shirked responsibility for the security of the bikes. Bugga!

In hindsight I was happier doing it myself if I'm honest. Securing the cargo net and giving my own directions to the geezer working the Derrick controls. Heart in the mouth moments watching your bike dangle precariously from the jib of the Derrick above your heads.

As I lashed them to the handrail of the forecastle I saw Heidi telling the Harbour Master to do one as she wasn't paying him for us to do it ourselves. She had a smile on her face as she did so p:-)

Cabin No. 1. Please. 1st class isn't exactly the Ritz but it's a cabin to ourselves. A far cry from the tent on the quayside.

Wow this was a flash back in time. All I could do was compare this with life on-board ship in The Marines. I can remember writing to my maw on the very first time going to sea.

If you don't have a roll in operating the ship you really do have to entertain yourself. The sway to and fro along with the underlying drone of the engine brought it all back to me. But ships routine was a bit different here. Not exactly ship shape and Bristol fashion but for Africa she was in a class of her own. A great chat with the ships Navigator. A genuine good guy with a wealth of knowledge and experience which put me at ease. Maybe not every ship needs to be like that of the Royal Navy.

Captains Rounds and endless chipping & painting. Mmm… the good old days…

We cover a number of topics from Scottish Independence to BREXIT. From African tea to you've got an easy life as a Mzungu Traveller.

Things to do were limited that's for sure but we entertained ourselves with the other Mzungus onboard in the galley. We were two of only four Mzungu (white people) on-board but good people all round. Jon a Belgian backpacker and Micheal a fellow biker from South Africa. Jon getting himself into some serious conversations with the crew. Being so close to the Congo you can only imagine that the

Hi Maw

The Bay of Biscay and it's like feeding time at the zoo… Blowing force 6–7 and the flat bottomed LSL (Landing Ship Logistics) is rocking and rolling all over the place. Metal Prison plates in hand as we cue for scran (food).

There's crash after crash of prison plates as slop is thrown to the Galley floor. Not all of it hits the floor though.

Heading for a table I was clutching my plate close. A Dutch Marine walks by with soup and custard dripping from his hair. Didn't laugh long though as it's wasn't long before my own is sliding down my leg leaving me stomping out my version of the Highland Fling for the lads…Not very hot then.

I remember that lesson now, "Never laugh at someone else's misfortune. What goes around comes around" They didn't laugh at me long, they all had their own plates to hold on to.

Think I'll be losing weight on here as they've closed the galley for the last 2 days, the weathers getting worse. Bread and soup from our metal mugs. Deep Joy!

There's lots chit chat and hanging around waiting for meal times. I've read my only book already. I spend most of my time jammed up on the top of the stack. Three bunks high.

Three's the magic number as there's only three showers for a mess-deck (dormitory) of Sixty. Its cosy!

There's a film on from forces TV most nights after Evening Rounds (inspections of the mess-deck) Idle hands and all that. They're always trying to keep us busy.

After the film they always put on a Tom&Jerry cartoon. Just the one, and everyone knows that's it for the night. Last night they forgot and no one left the galley. Mutiny because there was no Tom&Jerry.

Are You Laughing Yet?
Rough & Tough Marines eh!
I'll let you know how it all goes in Gibraltar.

Love to all
James (International Globetrotter and Renowned Storyteller)

locals remember the story of Belgium rule. Not the best of colonial times but he does survive his interrogation.

Scran or meal times were a flurry of activity. No cueing as there's waiter services. We don't mind that one. There's a choice. Take it or leave it and we can live with that too. At least there no prison plates but it is feeding time at the zoo. It's chaotic!... Nice memories...

There seemed to be several classes of ticket and cabins not to mention just sleeping up on deck so you had to tread lightly at times. Our cabin was a god send, a bolt hole for us to escape the ships routine. But it was almost routine to skip through fellow passenger lying on deck outside your door as you did so. I did feel guilty at times for being in cabin No.1 but there was always smiles as they look up from their prized spot on deck...

The Liemba is a real part of life to the Tanzanians living along the eastern shores of Lake Tanganyika. She runs down from Kigoma to Zambia then up again every two weeks calling at several townships along the way and not always at the quayside though.

Blow some soot and sound the horn and everyone for miles will know of her imminent arrival. Way anchor and let the hustle and bustle begin. Little boats are already on their way to meet and greet her. Some with passengers ready to climb aboard whilst others hoping for a chance of business. Whither it be a passenger looking to go ashore or the opportunity to sell some fish.

That makes it sound quite tame really but in reality it can be the absolute opposite. A stramash of adults clambering aboard and jumping off with every possession you could imagine. Kids handed down and hoisted up to anyone who is willing, whilst the little ones stay strapped in safety to mothers back. Packages of all shapes and sizes with various food stuffed in bags and buckets galore. Livestock, chickens and ducks to boot. All are passed to and from anyone willing to stick out that helping hand.

It didn't always go smoothly, people and goods did end up in the clear blue wet stuff but there was always plenty of those helping hands to snatch them back. Maybe a bit on the damp side but back they came, nothing and no one is lost.

Voices were raised, hands waved and arms flailed but to be honest they were merely argued about the price of fish...

Meanwhile the ships Derrick is busy unloading the cargo of the larger of the boats that surrounded her. Sacks of maize meal to be stuffed in the hold. Hey she was full to the gunnels when I climbed aboard so where do they find the space for it all. Who knows? but it does squeeze in.

She was something else! You could roll back the years quite easily and imagine the stories she could tell. I just can't believe she's over a hundred years old. Built by the Germans before WW1, transported from the coast to the lake in pieces before assembly. Scuttled by her crew during the war in fear of falling into enemy hand. But she never stayed there for too long as the best of the Royal Navy managed to re-float and restore her to working order after the war.

Old but not passed it yet, a credit to her crew that's for sure. She delivered us safely to kigoma where the mayhem of unloading began. For myself and the bikes I was quite happy to wait until the stramash was over once more. No easy way off for anyone as there was no direct gangway to shore. No empty berth so we had to use some old rusty tub as a stepping stone. Ok if you are a foot passenger but more heart in the mouth stuff if your bike is dangling from the jib of the Derrick once more. Not quite enough reach but there was a few more hands to help swing it!

Heidi's been paying our harbour fees whilst all this was going on so we're off and running. Woohoo...

Kigoma

Doctor Livingstone I Presume?

Probably one of the most famous lines ever when it comes to talking about Africa. Stanley, who was appointed by The New York Herald to search for Dr Livingstone. Well they met right here. Not right here as Ujiji is but a stone's throw along the lakeshore. It's said to be the oldest market town in Africa. So not just market day but **Market Town**, back in the day of the slave traders. Livingstone hanging around trying to change what was…

Ok not exactly hanging around, more recovering from his many excursions to the interior. Darkest Africa! White-man wasn't built for Africa then. Makes me smile when I think of it. We've already came across so many who've never met a white person. Back in the day I'm sure we'd have been more alien to the locals than anything else.

Strange blotchy white but almost red skinned creatures who hid from the days sun at almost any cost. Sickly and in need of rescuing from themselves. I know there was plenty who were well capable but many did pay the ultimate price…

Anyways a night in a cheap hotel and see what the morrow brings. There's no parking but that doesn't matter just bring your bikes in, so we did. So Africa! Not the best room we've ever had but all is good. The bikes are safe and we can hit the town.

Take a seat in a cafe at the side of the road and watch the world go by. Kinda cool, people watching. Hey they all do the same, not always watching where they are going. We've seen this before but no accidents thankfully. No swanky Thai restaurant for my lady this time.

Chips-my-eye instead. Precooked chips thrown onto an omelette as its flipped over to cook on the other side. Very tasty but just not that healthy. Try anything once, No? It's a part of life here as is sitting in the street cafe watching the by now almost intolerable African crap music on TV. Sorry Rap Music… OK it's not all rap music, but just not my cup of tea. Oh! and if I thought the music wasn't, then neither were the videos that came with it. Every cheesy dance step you've ever seen and almost every video the same. Mmm… Africa has shared so many gifts with us but this one I could have lived without…

A day visiting The Livingstone Museum

Christianity, Commerce, Civilisation. Livingstone's alternative hopes for ending the slave trade in Africa. Our journey thus far had criss-crossed his many expedition routes. Boyhood stories I do remember and this is undoubtedly the most famous. Underneath the Mango Tree, "Dr Livingstone I presume?"

"Yes... I feel thankful I am here to welcome you."

I'm not getting into the argument if that's what was exactly said between them or not. Livingstone had been out of contact with the outside world for six years. Just the mere fact that they were the only white-men for miles around was momentous. I was the only white-man to visit the museum that day. Presumably!

Sitting under Livingstone's Mango Tree makes me wonder. We (colonials) brought a mixed bag to Africa, and not all of it good...

But hey! this is market town, so make like a local. Thriving in many ways, full of everything. China that is! But there really was everything. Found ourselves rummaging through the piles of second hand clothes. We needed some gear for hiking in Rwanda. On the look-out for long sleeved shirts so why not make like a local.

The second hand clothes market is huge in Africa. Not all of our clothing donations made at the charity run back home, go straight to disaster relief. Just impossibly me thinks but so much ends up in the many market stalls the continent over. The second hand clothes market is massive and who am I to argue.

We just found ourselves doing as the locals do. If you want new clothing you can buy it at the china stall. If you want quality clothing then you do as we did and rummage.

We found three! A Dollar each. They'll definitely do to go hiking in. Two with the labels still on and probably never worn. Mmm... just have a think if there is anything in your wardrobe that still has the label attached and you might just never ware. Enough said...

We had a giggle and another night of people watching was on the cards...

The road to Rwanda was a dusty affair and one that remind us why we weren't taking the road through Burundi. More Aid Agency signs than I've ever seen. Several refugee camps along the road that hand railed the border. The road itself a buzz with women with bundles of firewood on their head to-ing and fro-ing whenever these camps were nearby. Unrest in Burundi and tensions are growing. A side of Africa that we don't always see. Maybe in more peaceful times...

18

Rwandan roads

It was like picking up a whole new book, never mind a different story! We hit the Rwandan border which in itself was space age for the African continent. Amazing! Slick friendly and easy to be honest, and we were let loose on the streets. Even the traffic seemed calm. Well, for a while.

From the border the countryside changed. Almost every inch is used for something. People are out working and with vigour. Something we've not seen in many other countries on this trip. Workers and hard workers at that.

Uphill, down dale. Hilly to say the least but stunning. Meander along the valley bottom and contour around the hill tops. Smiles, as we encounter three locals on bicycles hanging on to the back of a truck, towing them uphill. Became the norm overnight but if I lived and cycled here, I'd probably do the same. A bikers dream apart from the speed limit. No need to speed though. Not in a hurry but we still managed to have a local copper point his speed gun at us. We're cool!

The capitol was on us in no time. No longer farmlands but it was still built around the hilltops. A cool place.

I did say a bikers dream well maybe not. The city is full of the little Boda-Boda motorbike taxis. Only a few days here and things are spread around town. So if you want to visit the sights, then do as the locals do. My heart was in my mouth every inch of the way. Being a pillion passenger on a bike is something I don't do. This just brought it home to me. Not being in control!

Every bike in town was a TVS Boxer made in India. Not suggesting anything but not the best bike on the Global Market. Everyone wore a helmet and only two allowed on a bike. Truly ground breaking for Africa but it didn't make me feel any safer. White knuckle ride that's for sure. Think I'll be walking from now on I remember me saying. The Trick-cyclist laughing at the more experienced biker. Just not an experience I want to repeat…

A visit to the Genocide Memorial Museum. Sombre to say the least. What drives people in these times? It's not the only place it's happened over the years, but the fact the UN watched while they had boots on the ground is unbelievable.

70% saw someone murdered. 80% had someone they knew murdered, while 90% of the population actually thought they would be killed. Staggering!

Just couldn't go into the children's room in the museum. Tough Marine me. Yeah there's somethings that should just never happen… I'll leave that there.

Made me look at people in the street differently for a while. Can't work it out in my head. I'm not sure how anyone could work it in their head.

Put it aside for a moment and the people are brand new. Proud to be Rwandans not Hutu or Tutsi. We met nothing but kindness.

Met up with a local biker who was trying to help us find tyres that weren't Chinese. We failed but he was a good guy. Helpful and good company. He came away with a line I won't forget in a hurry as he told us about Rwanda.

It's the Switzerland of Africa.

Hey! he's not far wrong. More forward thinking than any other African country we've visited. Maybe starting with a clean slate and a little help from their friends might see them alright. More forward thinking initiatives here than most European counties.

Energy – Medical – Farming – Fishing – Recycling they do it all. But more than 50% of their GDP is foreign aid. Guilt Money from the UN you think? Who am I to judge.

The Congo Nile Trail was waiting for us over the next week or so. Neither along the Congo nor the Nile rivers but down the side of Lake Kivu. Out of Gisennyi, followed the northern shoreline south past the local brewery then meandered through little villages along the lake. A real roller coaster of a trail. Community campsites ran by school teachers and nights camping at the many coffee washing stations that are dotted along the route.

Tough for us as we've not really been off the bike for a while in fact only a few days hiking in Zimbabwe since being hit by the car in Windhoek. A good test for my foot me thinks. If I can't hack it here then there is no point in pushing myself anywhere else on this journey was the thinking.

Sore and stiff, especially in the mornings but I hobbled along until my aches and pains subsided. The Crazy-one not exactly finding it easy either. Work-Harder! Work-Harder!

The kids were pretty cool really but the sound of Mzungu Mzungu all day long got a bit tiring. Not sure you would get away with it if things were reversed back home. No malice in their words though. They walked along side or followed you along the trail. Sometimes I'd chased them for a giggle and they'd go running. They'd come back giggling and we get our camera out. Some would run but some would pose for pictures. Smiles all round really. Still makes me smile now.

We'd visit the local markets and stock up on crap. Sit in the local canteens and eat in the dark. Perhaps better that way but we ate it. Fuel is fuel. A great way to see Rwandan life at its basic. Well cool... trail life was tough but rewarding.

Farmers, pastoralists, loggers and plantation workers, there was lots going on. Most of it the old fashioned way. We past two men cutting a log with the you to me man-sized hand saw, one down in the pit and one standing on top. Wow, no need for a work out down the gym here.

Why am I complaining about my foot again? Enjoy the trail for what it is...

We pushed on to town. Kibuye. Nice enough and a good place to rest for the day. 91km hike and a 15km bus ride has took its toll. Feed me! Beer! Bed!

A day of rest and an early start the following day. 10km of Tarmac before we decided to call it a day. Lack of available information about the trail before we left, but it looks like the southern stretch has mostly or all of it been tarmacked by the Chinese recently. No fun for walking so we called it a day and returned to town.

[Video No. 28: **Congo Nile Trail**]

Weirdo

Well I said the people here were all good. There has to be the exception to any rule and we found it on our route out of Kibuye. Hiking along the road people came and went but one didn't. He just kept fallowing us. Keeping pace. Speeding up and slowing down. Just strange at first but when we stopped on the road bend he actually came back to have a look see. He tagged along with another who seemed to do the same then he turned off into the road construction site. Probably nothing but it made the hair on my neck stand on end. I won't be getting into a conversation with any of these two.

The trick-cyclist spooked as well. What would you do if you were on your own I asked? Taxi or Bus was the reply. Mmm…

More speeding up and slowing down with him doing the same. The final straw was when we decide to stop for a bit and he comes back up the road towards use. The Crazy-one not so crazy about this, looks and sound distressed, me too if I'm honest. That's enough as I go to grab my nunchucks. Remember what I said, there never really far away and I'm not gonna let anything happen to us. But hey! it was Heidi's hand that stops mine with a look and a no! OK?

I took a stance. Many years of karate had taught me never. Just never let anyone get within striking distance and this one wasn't either. What do you think you're doing? What you want? What's in the bag?

What's in the Bag? What's in the BAG? I kept firing questions at him and gave no quarter. His facial expression changed to one of fear. I had stopped him in his tracks. It was that fight or flight moment. He choose well. He chose the latter and made his way at speed down the road with the odd look over his shoulder. I'd have done the same if I was him but I wasn't following …

Fight averted but I found myself questioning my part in this.

No one gets within strike range if you're not sure of them. If he was innocent then he'll just go home and tell of the strange Mzungu he met on the road and laugh with his mates. If not he might think differently next time. Weirdo… Hey he's probably saying the same of me…

We did have a visit to the Environment Museum before we took the ferry boat back to Gisennyi. More proof that Rwanda is the Switzerland of Africa. The museum that is not the boat ride. This museum full of all things good in Rwanda.

The Ferry was a strange affair.

VIP ticket 5000 francs. Mmm… No thanks I'll have the normal ticket. I'm not sure what you got for your extra 3000 francs but I'm sure it wasn't worth it. You still got blasted with the same African crap music. Sorry rap music. Dreadful, but this lot had a twist of country and western too. Quite bizarre for these parts but it was still played at a volume the speakers couldn't cope with. Think I'm getting old or this could possibly be the worst music I've been subjected to in a long while. I definitely don't think so, as the music has been the worst part of our journey and not just here.

It didn't last forever as before long we had corkscrewed our way up the lake side. More to do with the boats dodgy steering than anything else. But it got us there.

In out of the rain and a well deserved pizza in Paradise. The Paradise Special with 2 Primus Beers please. A good end to the first section.

Over The Top

After another day of admin we headed for the hills. With our bikes this time. We decide to try another route south. Not along the lakeside but it was a real surprise that hit us as we turned off the road and headed up the track.

Narrower and narrower it got. Less traffic than we had seen for a while. Less and less people than we had seen for a while. The track all but disappeared. Covered over with grass where no traffic had passed but it was grazed by all the cows in Rwanda. Well at least some of them had been hiding out here. What a place. A cross between Switzerland and the Brecon Beacons in Wales. High hillside pastures with forestry blocks. What a ride dodging fallen trees and collapsed bridges. The trail was a real find. We certainly didn't expect it.

The Satnav did struggle in places as the rain threatened. Between the cloud cover and treetops it was interrupting our signal but I don't think either of us were really bothered how long it took. The trail was just awesome. A side to Rwanda we had missed so far. We did wonder where all the milk came from. Milky tea in the morning and milk everywhere you look really but the cows were few. They lived in style in the interiors wondrous high mountain pastures.

[Video No. 29: **Over The Top Rwandan Roads**]

The road came oh so soon enough. Back into Kibuye. Oops! the bikes leaking fuel. That can't be good. Fix it in the morning. Well so we thought.

Locked doors.

Up and at it. Well, after we found someone to let us out of the hotel. Totally locked up with no fire escape. Only in Africa! Stripped the carb out and cleaned out the bowl. Checked it over as well as I could. But I guess I'm not that good a mechanic. It still leaked out the overflow pipe. Drive on and try later as it doesn't leak whilst running.

Check the tyres and I need some air in the front. Idiot at the garage pulling at my valve as the compressor connection don't fit. Anyway off down the road for a bit but the tyres flat within half a kilometre. Never a good feeling when it's the front tyre. Tighten the valve and hand pump, I'll keep an eye on it.

It didn't take long, at the first dodgy corner and the front wants to through me off.

The valve has come away from the tube. That will be that then!:-)

Getting used to this tyre changing act (tyre monkey heaven) but this time all we have is the cheap Chinese inner tube. Mmm… a thorn and a piece of wire in the tyre too. That won't last. So we split the old tube and put the Chinese one inside. A bit of wriggling and in it went. I had a job pumping up my own tyre as the local lads tried to help. You just know what's coming when it's done. Yip! you must pay!

I didn't want the help but how do you stop them…

Anyway off up the road once more. 10km and the almighty back fire. Wow! The Crazy-ones bike running like it's fuelled on beans. But it's running so move on. Thought we'd avoid the rain but no chance. It caught up with us. Or rather hit us head on.

Shelter in the bus stop with the locals for a bit. Changed Shauns spark plug, but no joy to be honest. Get him to town as we can't do much in the rain. Cant? Maybe just don't want too. It's chucking it down in buckets, freezing too. Are waterproofs a must for Africa? Hell Yeah! Can't believe I ever questioned it.

Cyangugu. The end of the trail. Yip! covered in Chinese Tarmac. Glad we didn't hike it. A DRC border town but a night at the Catholic mission and all was good. Good food in the Restaurant across the street and a beer while watching the locals to-n-fro over the bridge to the Democratic Republic that is the Congo.

Oh! and the by now African routine of chatting up the blonde white chic even if she has her fella in tow. Yeah right in front of me. You gotta laugh but no harm really…

Intriguing The DRC might be but I'll leave that one for another day. Elections are due in the next few weeks and that's never the right time for pasty white tourists to visit. Blonde chic in tow or not…

Dusty Auld Bags

Up early once more and another attempt at the carb. Still no joy. Gonna have to do some research on this one.

Waterproofs on early as we head east and it's not long before we discovered why they call it the rain forest. Nyungwe Forest, Hey! it rains.

Wetter than a wet thing. Glad to get to town. Butare

Deja Vu, up once more with a plan to strip the carb down with a list of checks to do. How did man every live without YouTube. Float heights, needle valve and the likes. Wish we had pulled the jets out this time as it run worse than ever when we tried to start it.

Strip down once more. Out all jets and the primary or pilot one has a blockage. Managed to make sure it was clear this time. Put my fuel tank on the Crazy-ones bike and test fired it. What a relief. Dodgy fuel me thinks, we'll definitely have to ditch what we have. I'm sure someone will take it. Not much wasted around here me thinks.

Put it all back together and Shauns singing once more. No back fire on the test run either.

We've learned more about how the bike works in the last eighteen months than anything else. Good to learn even if we still have to ask the odd question to Jim back home. I'm sure he enjoys it even if his customer care skills are… Lacking shall we say… RPM Motorcycles, Falkirk's friendly motorcycle service!

If nothing else he'll get a laugh at us over his morning milk break in his workshop.

The day ran away with us but it was good to fix the bike ourselves. Just have to leave the visit to the cultural museum till the morning.

Got to visit something other than one of the many genocide memorial museums. This country has surprised us and we know that it has more to offer.

Ethnographic Museum Rwanda

A great insight to all things Rwanda. Well things that weren't connected to the Genocide. From the royal families hut of Kagondo to all things homestead. Wood carvings, pottery and metal worked weapons of old. Strange looking wicker ware hoods to the intricate hide/leather work. Very special me thinks, I suppose it's a leather thing. Well worth the entrance fee that's for sure. Rwanda's got more to offer in its historical past rather than the nightmare it is wakening up from.

Back just in time for the afternoon down-pore.

In stroll two British biker chicks. Shona and Pat, The Dusty Old Bags as call themselves.

Great chat and an invite out for dinner. Chinese meal would you believe? I know we'll meet these two again that's for sure. If nothing else, we enjoyed listening to their stories. Can't beat sharing a meal with new found friends.

They were off to Madagascar. Lucky buggers.

No peace for the wicked as we had a date with a Ugandan border guard. Not overly important which one. Anyone would do. Just need to get there. Easy riding to be fair.

Campsite come hostel on the outskirts of town and we were sorted for the night. Even had time for a beer. Needed something to take the edge off pre border-day excitement. Yeah I'm trying to tell myself it's excitement these days.

I shouldn't have gotten so excited as it was all low key and no real hassle. The only excitement was between the customs dude and the immigration official.

Don't tell me how to do my job! I've been in the game for 20 years. Ok!

Just don't take it out on me. But he was cool with us. A quick check of our kit and he was happy. We were happy too.

Stamp the carnet and some money changing. Hey! no hassle. Let's do one.

19
Uganda Ugly

A ride around the lake it seems. We were heading to a campsite on the other side with no real direct route to it (in my head I know what I mean). The track was merely a track and not really that inviting. So head around the road for a bit. Need supply's too, so a trip to the local super-market, always good.

Overland Camp.

We randomly pulled this one out a hat but what a find. The edge of Lake Binyoni. The edge of the lake was right enough. Couldn't get any closer. What a place. Well posh in its restaurant and Chalets. But as usual we took the campsite but we're rewarded with something awesome. What a beautiful site.

Chill here for a few days that's a must…

Only a couple of 4x4 from South Africa. Can live with that one. Then the tour bus gets back from its day trip Mmm…

Hey! we can't have it all.

A few days of rest and catch up with the outside world at our leisure. With a bit of Wi-Fi when we want in the restaurant and time for Heidi to catch up on a bit of writing. I'm happy just spinning my nunchucks to be honest. Got time to check the bikes over which is always good. I have a growing need to look after them as our journey rolls on.

The South African crew were cool too. Time to chat about the world and all things Africa. South Africans out and about doing their thing. These ones just a bit more travelled than most but good company.

The morning came early.

Don't know if it's me. Maybe I'm just tired or something but when you see the tour bus turn up you fear the worst. Hell we've been burnt before. The last night in feckin Zimbabwe with the Irish backpackers was brutal.

But give them their chance. These trucks don't stay anywhere for long. Just didn't expect the bastards to get up in the middle of the night and start the truck ready for the off.

04:10. Oh my feckin god. WTF

I Don't Believe It! Yey Victor they've started the truck. The Grumpy old man in me coming to the surface. Didn't last long but it was enough to wake me from my sleep. Spent the next hour drifting in and out of restless slumber. Listening to pots pans and ever other kitchen utensil known to man banging away.

All good fun if your for the off but not for us. At least not from where I was sleeping. Or Not!!!

Couldn't hold back when the truck started up once more. Lost the plot!

05:40

Your havin' a feckin laugh!

Straight to the point and no need for translation.

What are you all aboot? There's people trying to sleep.

I must! For the Brakes!

What you really mean is fuck everybody else I'm alright jack!

You ignorant c@^t! Yeah I used the C word.

Can't remember what else I called him as it was all I could do to stop myself from beating him to death with his pots and pans. When he put his hands on me I saw red...

Think the others did to. More people tried to get in between us.

I hope you're all leaving soon you inconsiderate bastards...

Off I went and got the security guard. But didn't have to go far as he was there in the back ground. Hiding most likely. Gave him a peace of my mind too.

Not much you can do really. Avoid the tour bus in future. They're all stuck in their own little world and don't give a fuck about anyone else. The most inconsiderate travellers I've ever come across. That's twice now and we really have learned the lesson. No more Tour Trucks!

Was off to make my feelings known with the management but no one in the office. Funny that must be something to do with what time it was. Ha-De-Da…Ha-De-Da…

Hey I cooled down a bit later. I now you need to pressurise the air brakes on a bus before you drive off but waking up the whole campsite 2 hours before you leave.

Just not on!

The management turned on the generator to power up The Keyboard Players laptop, to let her work so things weren't that bad.

Later listening to the South African crew telling stories about their trip to see the mountains gorillas it all seemed not to matter. We'd have loved to go but at $600 a skull we just couldn't justify it. Decided to keep the money for a trip to the Danikal down the road.

Someone else's stories were cool for now.

They left us to it in the morn and a campsite to ourselves. Nunchucka Circus and peace and quiet for the keyboard player.

Up and go in the morning. It's a fresh start with your batteries recharged.

Didn't get far down that road though and I've picked up a puncture.

It's not so bad but I could do without the audience. Must have been 30 kids around me. Hey! made for slick drills and it didn't take long.

Quickly turned off the main road and hit the gravel. Oh! the way we like it. Glorious track across the mountains. Little traffic and time to enjoy. Rolling gravel trails twisting away the hours.

Too good to be true though as I picked up yet another puncture. Bugger lost count now. 4? 5? Shit is this 6?

My rear tyre has just dropped off the cliff edge. After looking good for so long they really have come to the end of their life. Beginning to wish I had made a different decision in Kigali. Kampala isn't that far. Just have to keep it rolling.

Less of an audience this time. Only a handful of school kids to entertain. Just wish it wasn't so hot. Fighting with the extra hard mefos tyres in the blazing sunshine, just not good for your headache.

Need to drink more… The Crazy-one doesn't need to suffer my headaches.

Not far to the campsite. Or so we thought. It turns out it's as cheap to have a room. Or so we thought.

What a find. Nice new clean. In the shower and a knock at the door. The receptionist showed and charged us the wrong price. You should have paid the tourist price not the local price. Which just happens to be double.

Really?

I'll be leaving then. No! No it's ok we'll just charge the local rate. Mmm… the sign of things to come me thinks. If it was a proper government tax then I could kinda live with it but this just feels like being robbed.

Hey we're not staying, so up and at it in the morn. Don't care how nice they are. Treat me for who I am not some sort of walking wallet.

The road skirts the edge of Queen Elizabeth National Park with every chance of seeing some wild life. But only 500m out of town and there's elephant dung on the track. Oh it's fresh!

Can't stop scanning the side of the track but no sign of the big guy. Plenty others out there though from buffalo to warthog and back again. Just have to keep looking.

Weather changes again and on with the waterproofs. To think I was gonna send them home. Glad I didn't.

The road turned sloppy, muddy and wet all too quickly but we were treated to the distant sight of a dozen maybe 15 elephants in the distance. Only one at first but as we turned to check him out there was a whole family group just off to the side of him. Well cool. Didn't care it was raining then.

Keep looking around I'm saying to myself. Not getting caught out from behind but it was all happening in front of us. Another gift from Africa.

Push on to the road and immediately into traffic, kinda. Just a narrow bridge but we bumped into the South African Crew once more. Time for chin wag and a final farewell. They had just come from where we were heading.

The Equator…

Yip! the first sign of the northern hemisphere for a while that's for sure. Big round ring at the side of the road proclaiming so. But no peace for a photoshoot. Done the only thing possible and got the street kids involved. Eventually got one to take a picture with us both in it. Result! but not handing over me good camera. Not that trusting and there's always a hustle.

Onward to town and another campsite. Shower would be good after this one. It's the simple things in life that you miss while on the road and it's the shower I think I miss most. Well it is when I need one. Prayers answered!

The track becomes more of a road and the road becomes more and more busy, but we're on our way to Kampala. Capital cities not always fun and this one had a reputation, but after a few days of riding the steadily more congested roads, we hit the city ring road. We had survived the suicide bus drivers on more than one occasion on the way to town but what was around the corner was just bonkers. No rules, no respect for each other or the poor buggers that had to walk the roadside.

One twat sitting in the middle of the road buying a pair of jeans from a street vendor just causing mayhem. By the time I get there he decides it's time to leave. Runs his car right across me bows. Stuck my boot into his flank. Virtually no reaction. Wow it's the norm… your car's gonna be full of dents if you keep doing that to me… Did say something before about defending your road position. You gotta laugh though as I'm not sure they know any better. Do unto others and all that.

[Video No. 30: **Kampala kaos**]

A few days in the hostel and a run around town. Not that interesting to us, yeah! there's a host of restaurants and nightclubs but we can live without it. We'll give the Kampala nightlife a miss… but maybe that's the small town boy in me. We're so RocknRoll but they did have a Shoprite Super-market which meant rusks!

Sad I know but we'd become addicted to them and this was definitely the last call. The Crazy-one had even checked that one out online. Not that crazy eh!

Couldn't get my tyres either I'm afraid. It's gonna come back to bite me I'm sure. It all became too difficult making phone calls around town. Not speaking the lingo made it much harder. I'll have to make do till Nairobi. We did pick up our new Carnet de Passage from good old DHL so not a total failure. A sign of how long we've been on the road if it needs replacing.

Heading to Masindi

Humphrey Bogart & Katherine Hepburn had stayed here when filming the legendary film The African Queen. Good enough for them, then we can camp in the garden.

Suited us really. Pitched our tent in the pavilion with electricity and a shower and toilet block all to ourselves. The keyboard player could get on and I could tinker with the bikes once more. The nunchuckas or spanners in hand I don't mind.

[Video No. 31: **Hotel Masindi**]

Cool place and the gateway to Murchison Falls National Park.

This is where it got interesting. Every country we had travelled through did not allow motorbikes in the national parks. A fair point if you have lions or any other big cats running around.

Uganda? Well Uganda doesn't care.

Sure you can take your bike in the park!

Nothing else was said. No ifs buts or maybes. Crack on and do your own thing.

Stoked at this prospect…

Murchison Falls National Park

A days ride up the side of Lake Albert before you hit the gates. Stay in the choice lodge that's there. Well cool! Get some info about the park and get tickets in the morning. We sat, watching the rare sight of hippos out and about during daylight. Spent what was left of the day scanning up and down the water's edge with me monocular.

I swear blind I saw one having a go at one of the tour boats as it went by. Got a bit excited if I'm honest but it was only me that had the monocular.

Yeah! Yeah! I've seen it happen before… must happen more than you fink… but I swear it's what I saw… Mmm… sun setting whilst listened to the hippos out on the river. Sound familiar?

Taking the road around to the falls in the morning and a boat trip up the river in the afternoon sounds excessive but seeing them from both angles is what's best apparently. Took those who know at their word and wasn't disappointed.

The Falls were spectacular and deserted. No one on the track and no one on the trail to the top. We had them to ourselves. Just can't believe they're deserted.

Hey glad to have them that way.

Stunning, absolutely mesmerised by them. The noise the spray that vibration that runs through the ground giving you that feeling you'll be dragged in at any moment. The roar that is all consuming as the waters thunder bye. Hey! with an almost permanent rainbow climbing over them, this is a good day.

It wasn't over either. Off around to the ferry point for some lunch and check out where the boat left from in the afternoon, it was well chilled. If it was just lunch then I was stuffed and well pleased but sitting at the pickup point looking out across the river was mind blowing.

There must have been 50. Yip! Fifty elephants down at the water's edge for a drink come plunge in the river. My elephant count just blown out the water. Hey you know what I mean...

Sat in silence with the video camera running. Just couldn't believe my eyes. Africa is full of gifts!

20

The African Queen

I'm sure it was sunk by the Germans. No? Not the one of old, but a modern one for us tourist. Still we enjoyed the trip and the guide was a bit of a spotter so we did see loads of birds, hippos, monitors, antelope and warthog. More elephants and the odd croc.

Just magic.

Then the falls from a head on angle. Wow! Just Wow!:-)

The water is brilliant white as it crashes over the top before it drops into the coffee pot below turning it into that floating, foaming cappuccino. A constant stream of coffee coloured foam rushing down river from the falls as it churns up all before it. Ok not so clean looking, but not really dirty. Just disturbed the sandy bottom me thinks. But the roar and rush of the water was relentless. The boat fought against the current for as long as it took, allowing everyone to get their selfie. It's the way of life. Modern day graffiti up there on social media.

#I was here!# It is what it is! We did the same and loved it.

[Video No. 32: **Murchison Falls**]

Slow cruise back to the ferry point and not so much spotting. Just chill.

Dinner, Beer and early to bed. Big day and another one to follow.

Up early and pack in the dark. Want to catch the early ferry. Easy enough. There's always room for a little one. Hey! we had two, but it was just the same. They stuck us and our bikes up there on the off ramp. Right out in front. Be lying if I said I wasn't a bit scared. When locals are asking lots of questions about your bike and your journey it usually would disappear. But when there asking what you're gonna do if you meet a lion then it kinda stays with you.

Mmm... as long as I can out run The Crazy-one...

An old joke I know, but what you gonna do?

Rev the bikes head off and gun it, if it all goes Pete-tong.

Bravado maybe, but there is no right answer. There's no guarantee you'll react at all. Fright or flight you're definitely not standing up to the big cats.

Normally the wildlife avoid the noise of the bike so any time we see anything it's a bonus. We love to see the wildlife and not everyone gets to see it from the saddle.

A quick check of our pass on the other bank.

Asked once more where our guide was. Mmm... nope we don't have. Ok have a nice day.

Hey we're off and running.

Tried not to follow the crowd. There wasn't many really, but enough 4x4s that we didn't want to follow. We took the road less travelled. Hasn't done us any harm so far.

Giraffe Antelope Zebra galore then the Elephant in large numbers. Possibly the herd from the day before. So cool to see them like this. We did try not to disturb but when the track turns you in to their path. Because it is their path. Give them the right of way. A little to close for one of the younger males and he gives us a fake charge. Looked real enough but just a reminder me thinks!

We carried on and on aware we hadn't seen any of the big cats apart from ones in the sanctuary back in South Africa. Wasn't sure I was ready for running into the hyenas though. Only one but a pregnant female sitting close to her den.

Hy Hy Hyenas. Bugger I couldn't get me words out, but just encouraged Heidi to open it up. She was only meters from the trackside. I really didn't see her till we were right on top of her… One cat/dog thingy I can live without meeting…

Stopped for a drink and a sandwich at the waters edge. Not complacent. We watched our arcs. Plenty of open ground around us.

Dry as a bone. The excitement me thinks. You just don't get to do this every day…

Ready for more

We continue with fewer sightings of anything but what does that mean?

A 4x4 comes from the other direction asking about the lion. Then another asking the same but we had nothing to tell. Their driver suggesting we go the other direction due to the angry elephant down the track.

Mmm… how angry?

We had a look anyway.

It wasn't long before we were literally twisting and turning our way through the dung filled minefield.

Yip he was at the side of the track trashing the trees!

Not sure we're actually going down there. Back track and go around and if the lions are further down that track we're not meeting them today. The big guy has the final say.

Contented ourselves with buffalo and giraffe. Hey they were Rothchilds which made a difference. The best way to describe them is there colours are just that bit more vibrant than any of the others we had seen before. These were the trendies if you like. The smartly dress guys of the giraffe world. Very cool indeed.

Time had gone so quickly in the park. Something to do with being on your toes most of the day. But one last surprise in store.

Two Rothchilds Giraffes Necking in the middle of the track. This was worth watching. Just don't know how long it went on. Ok they might have been young ones just jousting and sizing each other up but not being an expert I just sat and stared. Eventually I did get the camera out knowing full well the little GoPro bike camera is just not gonna cut it at this range.

I say jousting but what it really looks like is some sort of dance. Using the track as their stage. A performance of grace rather than aggression. They circled one way then the other, necks extending out and swinging towards its partners one then the other. Too You, Too Me kinda action. I'm not sure what kind of damage is possible with those cone like antlers delivering blow after hammer blow but it was hypnotic to me.

We'd seen so much in just one day it was incredible really. The excitement of telling the story to each other of the same experience was strange. Hell we had seen the same picture but differently.

Won't forget this one in a hurry.

I said one last surprise. Not quite true.

Just before dark we reached the campsite just outside the gates at the other side of the park. We pitched the tent and took a beer on their balcony of the lodge. We were the only guests.

Out of the bush strolls a lone elephant. Doesn't really change his general direction but keeps strolling taking the best of the foliage the bush has to offer as he goes. He's going away from us but from where I'm looking as the sun is setting, Africa is good to us once more.

What a ride!

Kidepo Bound

It's gonna be hard to top that one. But hey! the memories won't ever leave me.

The road out in the morning is a mud bath. Everything sticking to the tyres and with my chain guard missing the crunch of stones running through the sprockets is cringe worthy. Wasn't sure I'd do some serious damage to the bike. A dreadful noise. We had to stop several times to clear out the stone fill gloop of mud from inside the engine sprocket cover. Eventually running without it, in fear that it would break. The road didn't come soon enough. But it came thankfully.

Make some distance. Heading for Kidepo National Park in the north.

A night at Fugleys along the way. Just another campsite but in town so we can ask about the roads and whatnot that lay ahead. Good people and good chat. Good advice too. Tom passed on all the good stuff about up north and where we should go. He did mention there was no camping but you can ask when you get there. A few more beers and a plan for the days ahead. Can't be bad.

Kidepo Lodge

The road out of town dwindled very quickly into a gravelled track. Did I mention? it's the way we like it. It's never a chore if we can still stop and take pictures and video. Even track back to take them isn't a chore.

We weaved our way through the bush with the track to the Kidepo gates. Not much of a gate but we said hello and had a chat with the guard. No problem if you're staying at the lodge.

Well no camping is what we found and no bending of the rules but the beer was good.

No bluff, we would have gone and slept in the bush but there was a discount waved in front of us. So a night in the old style safari tent with its own shower and toilet. Glamping, African Style. Happy Days.

Great chat with the owner and his guests. A kudu researcher and a mechanic fixing his generator. Glorious evening with chat of the old days. Yeah the border regions have had a troubled past. Civil war, poaching and the likes but you can't take anything away from its raw beauty…

Looking at the mountains across the border in South Sudan and Kenya whilst sitting on your porch in Uganda. Africa is good to us once more.

Rolex

We'd loved to have stayed. We'd loved to have gone deeper in to the park but the journey goes on.

Up and a walk out with Bill. He knew so much and told us more than we could remember about the park and its surrounding. It was his sons place really but what a place. Truly Stunning.

A run into town before turning South and Kenya. No South Sudan for us this time. There is still unrest there so just no point in fighting the issue.

Supplies and a Rolex for the road.

I had seen the Rolex sign at the side of the road before and never questioned it but Maria the American Kudu researcher says it's a must. Road food but road food at its best.

Spanish omelette rolled in a chapatti kinda thing. What's her name? Truly Scrumptious… Yeah I remember Mary Poppins….

We're the subject of everyone's interest in town but it's Happy Town and the Crazy-one wants fed. The crowd grows around us but we're not an everyday sight round here, eh! All is cool.

Easy road around the mountain and what we hope is fuel. Not running out but you can't be sure when the next fill up is gonna be. All is good as we reach the fuel station in town, there's a guy standing at what looks like a modern pump, but there is no electricity. So he's hand pumping it. Needs must and all that.

Down the trail in search for a quiet spot and a camp for the night. Not so easy but we think we've cracked it. It only takes 5mins though and someone appears.

He sits up on the embankment just looking. I wave he waves back and that's it.

Nunchucka Circus. Hey it's my thing these days. After another ten minutes of me showing my stuff he gets up and goes around the back of us. What no applause? Out of sight so I head on up the embankment a little further than before. We did check around us before pitching the tent but seen nothing.

Mmm… Some sort of village. Mud brick built Rondavaals.

Let's just wait and see.

Didn't wait long. Three guys in some sort of military get up. Only one gun but one of them did have a radio. Oh bugga! What's this?

Turns out it was some sort of military camp. Didn't look like one to me, just not what I can remember them looking like but hey it was. They were cool with it after I gave them our explanation. Promised we'd be gone in the morning. Can't go anywhere now it's nearly dark.

The heavens opened up once more and that was that they all bugged out and left us to it. Never heard anymore until morning.

Never bothered with the morning cuppa though. Never like the audience me. Especially one with a gun.

Packed up the tent and waved good bye. It's all go… another easy day on the trail? You can live in hope…

Heading for the Suam River Border Crossing but we're in no hurry. There should be a campsite if we need it. A bit like the forestry commission but who knows. Just take it as it comes. The Road was good enough for now. But at the first check point the coppers looks confused and asked why we weren't going this way, pointing up a side track. Ok if we must.

Up the hill like a local, the track was a bit tasty to say the least. Glad to see locals coming down with a load on. It gave me confidence that we'd make it up.

It was good enough but we're glad to turn on to the bigger track up top.

Into the village and time for a Rolex. OK not the healthiest but bloody tasty. Much better than the chips-my-eye thingy. As always there's a crowd with in minutes. A group of young lads checking out the Trick-cyclists ass as she checks her tyre pressures. Followed by the usual chat her up routine. I make a comparison with her patchwork jeans and those of Romeos camouflaged baggies.

Hey, look black guys get red-faced and embarrassed too. As he then becomes the target of everyone's attentions. It makes me smile… but no harm done… Smiles around.

The road gets steeper from here and its up and over the top. The only thing with over the top is that the clouds that gathered there.

Through the forest it's getting darker by the minute but no sign of the campsite. Mmm… Ask a local about a guesthouse and the usual.

Hand waved in a vague direction. In my mind he doesn't know but just won't admit it. Can't loose face. We go on and on and it's really is getting darker. We stop and look at each other. Feck neither of us knows. It might be the tent but where. All forestry blocks and fences. Sometimes just not that easy to get off the road.

A local rides up on his Chinese steed. You're here pointing at the trees. Oh! Ok?

But he was right and there was even a sign. Not a bloody big sign but there was one. Let the Crazy-one do her magic and she ran off to find someone. She came back with a lady who says it fine to camp as the guesthouse is full. Cool where? Before we could... you know what happens.

We all make a mad dash for the cluster of buildings on the other side of the road. Pishin Down.

Offered the outhouse barn type building or fend for ourselves. No brainer really. We'll take the barn. Well, we'll take the barn when the rain stops.

Hey! friendly chat with the park rangers. They're all good as everyone is taking shelter in their main office block.

The rain eventually did subside and we pitched our tent inside the barn. Cozy night.

No hurry in the morning as things a sodden wet. The suns out and drying the track. We've been caught out on the Ugandan Snot covered tracks before. It's like Bambi on Ice. And not in a fun way. But by the time we're sorted, so is the track and the ride over the top is a joy. It doesn't take long to dry out really.

Down to the border post and see what happens.

Guy at immigration.

Where you from? England & Scotland.

Ah Arsenal? No?

What team do support?

You heard of the mighty Glasgow Rangers?

Of course, I was brought up a Protestant. There my Scottish team. Result!

In you come. You want cup of tea?

Sometimes travellers stories are just full of the horror that is border day but this one was a breeze. Cool one at that.

21

Kenya

Over the border and it's busy. Much more busy than we like it. I knew it would be so. We're heading for Nairobi and the road only gets bigger. First Eldoret then the Lake Naivasha.

Eldoret came quickly as we ran the edge of the Rift Valley, well kinda. But it was cool enough. Still we could do without the crazy traffic.

A night at the posh campsite. Cheap enough for what you got but the beer? Twice the price of anywhere else. A sign saying Bill Gates stayed here! Really! Who cares? Nice place but the overpriced beer? Must have been the Bill Gates thing. Does he even drink beer? It was a means to an end so we passed through.

We could probably make Nairobi that day but the decision was taken out our hands by yet another puncture.

The rear once more. Just can't remember what number this is and **oh dear!** There is a split in the tyre too. You know it's bad when you patching the inside of the tyre with an old inner tube and the threads are showing through what's left of the caucus.

My usual audience at the side of the road but they were good. Fellow bikers them all. All be it Chinese bikers. What I mean is bikers who ride bikes from china. Remember the Chinese scooter revolution thing.

I did say a long time ago I'm not stopping for every broken down Chinese scooter the length of Africa. But I've never not stopped if they had a puncture. That's just the evil that is. Gave away my patches and glue on a few occasions. It was nice that they stopped for me.

They didn't have any puncture repair kit but it's the thought that counts. No?

We did get to the lake before dark so all was good. A beer was on the cards as a reward me thinks. We were so close to the safety of the city and some new rubber boots for the bikes. It didn't take long for that reward to take effect and in the tent. Dreamland won't take long me thinks.

You won't get to sleep too quickly though. The security guards running down in the direction of the lake with their torches flashing and whooping as they go.

WTF? Hippos.

They ran for it and then the splash. They wouldn't have ran if it was daylight.

Made me smile and we cuddled, listened to their grunts for a while before dreamland.

Up and at it. Nairobi awaits but there's a Danish couple on BMWs on the other side of the campsite so time for a chat. They had just come down through Ethiopia so we defiantly wanted to chat to them, that's for sure.

There's unrest and a state of emergency declared. It was all kicking off as they rode through. Maybe not as bad as the papers would lead you to believe but it was happening. They said they were fine with what was going on. Demonstrations all aimed at the government. The only thing that was aimed at them was the kids and their stone throwing. Mmm... we had heard of that several time.

They'd shortened their stay but at the end they would have been happy to stay longer.

Can't be bad then. A swap of shipping details. You can't have enough options for the end game and a cheerio. No not the breakfast thingys. Goodbyes...

Nairobi

Out onto the road but not the main one. The back road into town.

168

Up and over the mountain. Switchback heaven. Well it might have been if it wasn't for the nutters that wanted to run you into the gutter at any chance they got. Shit it's just no funny...

Jungle Junction

Nairobi is a growing city and like all in Africa trying to run before it can walk. There is chaos on the streets. Bonkers, just bonkers and when it all ground to a halt, ride like a local and take to the pavement.

Yip just Bonkers!:-)

It wasn't just taking to the pavements. Roundabouts and traffic lights didn't work either. Coppers at all entrances to the roundabout holding back the flow. Scooters weave their way to the front of the cue and as soon as he turns his back there off. Amazing! Well amazing how long it took us to blend in. Not long really!:-)

But it was good to get to Jungle Junction...

Sanctuary within the city. Kristoff was a motorbike traveller of old. Travelled through Africa many years before, he just got stuck here.

He had it all. Food, beer, Information, a workshop and a great place to stay. Managed to service the bikes. A journey into town and pick up some new boots for the bikes. Mitas tyres, my prayers had been answered. Some awesome rubber for whatever lies ahead.

Not all go! We had been into the Ethiopian Embassy the day before only to told that to get an overland visa you had to be a Kenyan citizen.

Mmm... the consular had been nice enough to us but being female she was more talkative to the Crazy-one. One of these moments to take the back seat. I was used to every male police chief border type official missing me out and speaking to the blonde haired lady. This one just a different twist.

Go see the Ambassador was her advice. So we did. No personal audience just leave your passports, your papers and told our story to his flunky. She might have had a title but I wasn't confident. Phone back tomorrow. Mmm...

Hey tomorrow came and no real answer when we phoned. Come in this afternoon. Not even sure we had progressed any. Had he agreed to issues a visa? Had he even read our story? I left it to blonde haired one to go find out. Jimmy had new tyres to wrestle and fit.

The Ambassador had agreed to granting a visa but that meant filling in all the paperwork without me. But Heidi managed, submitting the forms and paying the fees. She even came back with a three months visa. Don't know how she did it but sometimes women speaking to women works in your favour. Well cool, we had time to enjoy a bit more of Kenya before hitting the border.

22
MasiLand

We've heard a load of scare stories about this road and we were keen to avoid it. Which we did. Well as much as we could. We chose as many of the little roads as was possible. Eventually looking South down the road at Mt Kilimanjaro in the distance. We were just gonna turn off the road and camp but as usual homesteads everywhere. Decided to check everything was alright with the locals. Sometimes it's just better that way...

It turned out we had stumbled across the local church with a meeting in progress. But everything was cool just pitch your tent here and we'll check on you later.

So we did, and they did.

More than just locals. Pastors from as far as Nairobi. There was lots of good chat and well wishing. Exchange of details just in case we needed help. Not that there seemed any need as this was Masi Country, all good people.

The road through the national park was not open to us so we had to do what we were trying to avoid.

The Mombasa Road

You're rolling along and the traffic slows almost to a halt. There's nothing wrong just some truck driver buying anything from oranges to onions from the street sellers. Never really stopping but rolling. This happened almost anywhere but was rife in between village traffic calming humps or just on the crest of a hill as the bigger traffic slows.

At times it was fine but that never really lasted long. It was never long before you were bullied by anyone who was bigger than you. Sometimes blatant disregard for their fellow man, sometimes just Murderous Bastards!

Some of the biggest wind turbines I'd ever seen being transported from the coast in sections. More chaos and cues of traffic begin to form. That's always a winner! These were huge!

If you have a cue of a dozen cars and the guy at the back just pulls out, drives his car straight at you. WTF?

Yeah! exactly what I thought on many an occasion. Enough said, you have to keep your wits about you.

We were glad to turn off it before Mombasa for sure. Nights here and there as we wiggled up the coast towards Lamu.

Stopped to check out the old Swahili settlement of Gedi. We hadn't come in contact with much on the road north along the coast but this was worth stopping for. Well worth the visit.

Abandoned long ago but the ruins were a great look into the past. A Swahili trading town of old. There's a few of these running up the east coast of Africa and a great glimpse of what used to be.

The road was quiet enough apart from more check points than before. Security seems to be the priority around these parts but we don't feel threatened. Maybe it's us they're worried about… but maybe not. We're getting closer to the Somali Border.

Not too far from the road is one of the biggest refugee camps but no real sign telling you so. Not that you would be allowed to go. In fact warned so, by a fellow traveller back at Jungle Junction.

It's noticeably poorer around here. As we stop for something at a roadside cafe we're instantly a target for the touts and fixers. You need anything food, shop, petrol, somewhere to stay there will be someone to help for a few coins. No harm really but I'm sure I can find what I want, believe me. If the Cray-one needs fed I'm sure she'll work that one out! Believe me!

We had become accustomed to the simple life of rice & beans with chapatti bread and this place was no different. It was what it was and we're no different from the locals. OK the white skin does attract more attention. Blend in, tear off a piece of bread and dig into your rice&beans with your hands. We're no snobs…

As we leave there is a crowd around us. Touts, kids, the curious and as I'm busy turning my bike around I hear the commotion. The Trick-cyclist has managed to crush a kitten that's been hiding under her bike. Oh Dear!

There's jeers, shouting and hands out. I'm not sure but was it in the hope of compensation or just the usual hands out in hope. Thomas our cafe fixer drags it to the gutter and waves us on our way. Chasing the hands of the crowd away.

I can still remember the Lesotho Puppy and how I felt afterwards. Not good. Heidis face says it all… Don't think I'll be bringing this one up in the future… let it lie… We've all had our moments…

Although we'd been riding north for a few days and it was never far away we hadn't really seen the coast. It's wasn't far from here and we'll have to find somewhere for the bikes if we want to visit Lamu.

No problem really, ask at one of the few cafes in the small town before the ferry and they'll send you to the only guesthouse.

23

Lamu Labyrinth

Wow! we wanted to hit the East Coast of Africa and we did with a visit to Lamu.

Finding somewhere to stow the bikes for a few days was easier than expected.

Just rent a room in a cheap hotel and dump your kit inside, park your bike in the courtyard. 100 yards from the police station. Can't get much better than this. Ok, there was a bit more to it than that but after a bit haggling the bikes can have a holiday from us.

Boda-Boda bike taxi to the ferry point. Not my idea of fun. Still traumatised by the Rwandan Boda-Boda taxi experience but he got me there in one piece. Needs must and all that so it can't be bad.

We took the slow ferry with the locals. In fact he came back for us. He had just shoved off but a fare is a fare and in this dog eat dog world we weren't being given up to the speed boat drivers that easily. Back he came and we jumped from the jetty. Easy does it.

And an easy ride down the water and Lamu.

Up the steps and fallow the instructions from Arthur, our host at the guesthouse. It got us wondering as we twisted and turned down the narrow street to the Jambo House. The tiny streets and alleyways were to become a thing of fascination in the days to come.

Jambo House was run by a German guy, Arthur. Full of facts and helpful with all things Lamu. He knew the place and made it his job to inform you too. The welcome briefing was very efficient as you would expect. Did I mention he was German?

A walk around town and the local fort. The Main Street. Well more the widest of the narrow streets but hey! we'll call it Main Street if you want us to. Then an organised tour of town with Achmed. No not the one that Jeff Dunham put his hand up from the rear. Local tour guide that really knows his stuff.

[Video No. 33: **Lamu Labyrinth**]

The difference of what was Old Swahili and what was Arabic around town. Great tour to be honest. He took us to every nook 'n' cranny there was. Houses being renovated. He took us in. Workshops, no problem they'll let me in. He seemed to know everyone.

Well worth paying a few quid now and then, that's for sure. A wealth of information.

All that and the list of places Arthur had sorted out we were exactly that. Sorted!

Great food and fruit juice heaven that's for sure all mixed in with the relaxed chilled out attitude. This place was magic...

No hassles from the locals not even the ones that were selling stuff. Hello how are you and a quick chat. I'm here if you want anything. Normally everyone has an angle. Kinda cool and refreshing for Africa.

Spent my evenings watching the stars from the rooftop terrace. Hey! it felt like we were on holiday.

Up and off to the beach well in slow time. A few kilometres walk but we were game. Just follow the waters edge minding the tides and it's easy.

Beach deserted with no one in sight and I mean no one. Strolled around searching the pools for starfish and when that was done we just sat in the surf.

[Video No. 34: **Shaela Beach**]

We're not sun worshipers or beach freaks but this was kinda cool. Could get used to this holiday stuff.

More time sitting on the roof with the new Super-moon. Never seen it so bright or as big for that matter. Found myself checking its rise & fall along with its whereabouts, trajectory thingy.

Such a cool space.

Easy days but we were looking forward to a Dhow boat ride later in the day, so as to catch the tide to the ancient Swahili village across the water.

Easily sorted with others in the guesthouse. A Kenyan guy and a German student. So just the four of us. Big enough number in my book.

Effortless Dhow boat journey to be sure. Her slanting triangular sail bellowing forwards carrying us across the main channel. Gliding through the mangrove on the other-side to the jetty at the ancient abandoned Swahili settlement. She's a bit fatter about midships than most around here but befitting those dhows from more southern water of Mozambique. Yeah! her skipper was a wealth of information too…

A tour of the old Swahili settlement dating back hundreds of years. A real throwback in time. I've never been such a historian. Never been told so many stories me thinks. Not as big as the Gedi ruins but every bit as thought provoking.

No time to linger though. A brief visit as the tide waits for no man. But what was in store was worth it.

Navigating our way through the mangrove we tacked to and fro across the water. Effortlessly skipping from one bank to the other. The Mangrove alive with a collection of screeching and calling of birds from all around. Gently easing ourselves back into the cushions to enjoy what was. The sun is setting and the views are just stunning. Maybe it's just my in-ability to describe it but I can't do this justice. It's a wondrous sight…

Waters turn from an almost calm as you turn out onto the seaward channel we had to cross. Slowly gathering momentum the ripples grow larger as the wind steadily builds. Not behind us but enough as to make the deckhands work at tacking the Dhow to and fro across the ever widening channel. Everything changing colour as we go. The suns a setting and we're gathering momentum. Finding it difficult to sit still it's hard to know which direction to point me camera. Need more cameras! Maybe not. Just sit back and enjoy it. Think you miss so much as you're busy staring down the view finder of the camera. Just chill.

Wondrous! Beautiful thing the Sunset, it always does but not always around to enjoy it at home. It passes you bye as you go to and from work in our everyday lives. Sure I've seen plenty at home but never always have had the time to enjoy them… One of Africa's gifts to you…

Dinner with our shipmates and yet another night on the rooftop. Could bring our bed up here and be happy. Another night of The Super moon. It's when a Full Moon coincides with a New Moon (perigee). The biggest it's been for nearly 70 years. A real gift as it's unlikely to be as big for years to come. Probably not in my lifetime…

In a flash our holiday is over. For it really felt like one.

Riding my bike's not a chore that's for sure, but Lamu was a real pleasure…

Bugga the list of places to go back to is getting longer…

The ride back to Nairobi just won't feel the same…

The Holiday is Over

Just couldn't handle a re-run of the Mombassa Road. We decided on a more northern route. Heading back the way we came until the check point at Minjila. They were happy enough to let us go north. Well after every man and his dog had their tuppence worth. A sign of their ongoing struggle with Al-Shabab and the subsequent refugee crisis.

They warned us off about all things bad around there, but let us go… up the road towards Garissa.

Can't say we really enjoyed the trail for that's all what the road turned into. The tarmac just broken everywhere and eventually disappeared. Locals collecting rain water from the puddles that had formed on and at the side of the road. Kids, mothers, just about everyone was doing it. A sign of how dry it is around here or is it the poor infrastructure and investment by them in Nairobi. Maybe another sign of the troubled times. A far cry, from the holiday we've just had. Back on the road eh!

We rolled steadily northward towards Garissa, not heading into town as a night in the bush should do. If truth be told I for one wasn't sure we'd meet with a friendly face in town. Not all in these parts are happy with the west and their ways. Doesn't matter which way you put it, Al-Shabab has a far out-reaching arm here in Kenya. Just don't think I'll be having a peaceful nights sleep. Heard everything that went down the track and more, that's for sure. Hey! there's good people everywhere in this world but I'm not up for putting that one to the test right here. You can think of me what you will.

Hit the main road in the morning and turn west toward Nairobi we ran straight into the military checkpoint. Think we caught them by surprise, for there's not many Mzungu tourist travel this road. They were chatty enough though. Found ourselves in a roadside cafe for breakfast with the checkpoint Capitan. Not really sure of his rank but I was sure he was in charge. Some people just have an air about then. Anyway I'm sure he sent word down the road as we had an easy ride heading west…

24
Journey to the Jade Sea

Still feeling miserable. Yip! the blonde haired white chick would have you believe it was man-flu, my head just not in the game but it was time to move on. Visa clock ticking and insurance deadline to think about. If we cross the border at the right time we can renew there perhaps, or it's not long until Addis Ababa. For sure we can do it there. Everyone and everything screaming at me to get out of my deathbed...

Raining and out on the ring-road. Not good but a necessary evil. An easier day it turned out to be if I'm honest and a cheap hotel at the end of it. Seen virtually nothing of the mountains for the clagg. Hey! it was to get better.

The weather cleared the following day and things began to change.

The road for a start. Turned off that at Archers Post and took the gravel road to Maralal and the Camel Jockey Club. A night in the bush along the way. Just by the sounds of it I'm expecting things to change. Things are a bit more arid in places and for sure it's heating up. A few military check points along the way but nothing to worry about. It's just the bush.

Switchback after switchback as we climb towards the plateau and a chance encounter with jumbo running across the road. Brilliant! bloody brilliant, as there is not power in either camera battery. An opportunity missed but a nice memory that's for sure. Wasn't sure what wildlife we would see out here. Never thought it be the Big Guy...

Hit the camel club quite early, well early enough to run into town for some supplies and a look see. Found a good bakery and stirred up a load of interest from the locals. Not many Mzungu travel through here. Crowds gather outside the mini-market. Met by a couple of missionaries from Scandinavia, Finland me thinks. Working in the community to translate and formulate a local written language Bible. Not everyone's cup o' tea but hey! they're willing to sacrifice their careers for what they believe in and they're out here doing it...

A warm beer and a chilled out evening. Getting ready for what the morrow will bring.

The unknown, but a nice chat with the campsite owner telling us how things have changed since he was young. He gave us the 2 wife's story, about Samburu and Masi. A nice story of a man with two wife's named Samburu and Masi who are coming out of Ethiopia in search of good water and a place to graze their animals. Two very similar ethnic groups settling in different areas. Samburo on the shores of lake Turkana and the Masi on the lower slopes of Kilamanjaro and the Serangeti. A story which has been handed down over many generations. There is a smattering of truth in it somewhere. Believe what you will.

Brought back memories of the book we read the summer before. "Journey to the Jade Sea" by John Hillaby. A journey of old as he travelled on foot with camel train following close behind. A different kind of dreamland.

On to Baragoi

No camels for us but I'm sure our little bikes will do just fine. Fuel and another gravel road heading out towards the lake. Great scenery once more but rugged and dry. There is fuel in Baragoi which alleviates most of my fears for the days to come.

In years gone by there was some 1100km between fuel stops on this route. Fuel here brings it into the little Serows range. Well with a few plastic bottles strapped to the side we'll be good. Even then I'm being cautious. Better to have and not need me thinks.

Our fuel finder, finds us a cafe for chi and chapati. For a small fee but he does keep our bikes safe while we're inside. A small price to pay for peace of mind.

The road once more and all that brings. One more village before the lake. Maybe a campsite and a shop. It has both but nothing much to sell. The locals don't have much. The whole area has been in drought for months. Loads of kid asking for water but there not really thirsty. Just a way of distracting you to get money or something else, anything else. They never stop asking. Nothing to spare I'm afraid. We need what we're carrying.

We bounce out onto a seriously upgraded gravel road coming from the east. It's upgraded for a reason.

The missionary's back in Maralal told us about the wind farm project. Bugga me I didn't expect this. But after the turbines we'd seen on the Mombasa Road, I should have known.

365 turbines in one of the windiest of places in Kenya. Impressed no matter how ugly they look.

I remember Hillaby stating how the Upepo (The Great Winds) effected his efforts. The winds would "began to rise at dawn until at times it had some of the skull-wrinkling intensity of a scream." The wind wasn't screaming at us but it had potential.

What it really was is the Turkana low level Jet. The wind from the east passing through the Turkana Channel running between the Ethiopian and Kenyan highlands. An ideal site then for the positioning of the wind-farm.

Hopefully the local villages will be hooked up to to grid when it comes on line. That will change the villagers lifestyle that's for sure. Progress is happening whither they want it or not. A truly massive project so l only hope they benefit from it.

More gravel but it can't be far to go. Then all of a sudden it's upon you. That beautiful blue green of the Jade Sea or Lake Turkana as it's now know. Gone is the old colonial name of Lake Rudolf and returned to something, more traditional. I'm sure there is no one around here who remembers the estranged Crown Prince of Austria.

We roll nearer to enjoy the view before us. Sit for a while and just stare into the blue green of the sea. Windy to say the least but truly beautiful. The colour's taking centre stage as the skyline of the mountains just fade into obscurity a long with the rocky outcrops all around us. Time to move on though and down to the lakeside track.

Kids come running to meet us as we get there. A huddle or manyatta of gadgees grouped between the waters edge and the track. All waves and smiles but hands out of course. They've probably lived that same lifestyle for many a year. Small and igloo like, stick framed skeleton shelters covered in animal hide. Fishermen and pastoralist for their lot. For what little pasture there was. Still amazes me how goats can thrive/survive on so little.

Thrown back in time, for what lay before us must have been the same virtual sight for many a year.

Loiyangalani and Camp Oasis

Over the hill stands an enormous antenna, must be the place. But over the top of the hill and stunned by the number of gadgees laid out in front of us. Amazing but just not what I expected.

Palm trees on the far side of town gave away the Oasis location. Lush as any a place we had seen. Watering the grass as we turned into camp. Set up our tent and a cold beer is on its way. Heaven in a bottle who'd have thought it…

Within the hour I'm being crowned the Rain King by the locals as I've blessed them by bringing it to them. I've been cursed for being Scottish and bringing it with me before but not thanked for blessing them with rain. (It did rain 6 out of 10 days out of Nairobi) I'll go along with the Rainman or Rain King titles for now.

[Video No. 35: **Lakeside Rainman**]

184

A days rest before we must push north. Managed to find more fuel (at a cost) to top up our fuel tanks here. Plastic bottles but it's clean. A true sign of a changing Africa. Where ever there is the Boda-Boda bike taxis there is fuel. A true Chinese revolution this far.

This should take us to a fuel station on the Ethiopian side rather than having to go to anymore of the black market dealers along the way.

Hobo Style

Up the lakeside hugging the shore line for a while. The blue green of the sea mesmerising us as we go. A never ending photoshoot…

The water level has dropped over the years so the shore line has shifted in places. Making for dried up inland mini lake-beds which have turned into grazing pastures. Not much of pasture but a lush sight for round here and a welcome one for the goats that are forced to endure this way of life.

We follow the trail north, passing close by to many small settlements and villages. Not always great in numbers but a fair few of them. A single set of 4x4 tracks veering off at every one then re-joining at the other side. It took most of the day to find the truck that left the tracks. An older style land-rover driven by some camouflage clad official types. Checking on the locals me thinks.

The sandy tracks get worse in places. Enough to spoil your ride that's for sure. Around a rocky section then back close to the waters edge. The sand is never far away getting softer and deeper. In fact up to the belly pan of the bike in places. Can get off the bike and leave it standing upright. Bugga I can remember saying I didn't want this again. Heidi had to come and push several times. The locals choosing to watch us struggle. They're probably dumbstruck by our own stupidity.

Hey! it won't last forever…

More and more herders. Goats donkeys and then camels. Things are changing. Then the biggest camel train I'd ever seen. I tried counting, getting to 150 before I lost count. So maybe 200 plus. What a sight as it slowly and purposefully snaked its way through the scrub…

Turned inland for a bit around the mountains that block our path. Not much daylight left so we had a decision to make. We decided to check out the next riverbed. Hey! an island in the middle of a dried up bed. Made tea and sit it out for a while. See what happens. Kids are round for a look but don't come near. Herders are around and only wave and go by. Oops! local Militia turn up to have a chat.

Ok, a local guy. Barefoot, US camouflage top with old British 58 pattern webbing carrying a Belgian FN rifle over his shoulder. We make out the word Askari and he seems to be semi – official. Askari being an old colonial term for native soldier. He's the most official type we've met around these parts.

We go through the camp for the night routine and he's cool with it. We're on his patch and everything safe here. He wonders off and we see another local approaching. They sit and chat with each other at a distance.

Jackal goes scurrying by… Gunshot… Mmm…

A short time later the kids go by carrying a goat that's been killed by the Jackal but it's not going to go to waste.

Over the next few hours I think the entire village came around to see us. All 8 of them. Some trying to speak others just come for a look see. But all good. Another offer of help from the local Askari. Water if we need but we don't want to be a burden.

One more visitor as it gets dark, a local camel driver stops for a few moments to check us out without saying anything. I'm sure he spoke to our Askari friend as he passed his door. Starry-Night Hotel and a good nights sleep.

Up and at it in the morning, well when the Trick-cyclist can drag herself out of bed. Some of the locals come to say goodbye. Well, a few kids and our Askari friend wrapped in his blanket. All good though.

[Video No. 36: **Camping Hobo Style**]

Off to the park

Sibiloi National Park, it's not that far to the park entrance and some up to date info we hope. A slow hot start to the day but a good trail. Not too sandy and we can make some headway. Had a chat with the guys at the gate to the park taking some pics of their map and they gave us some cold water. Good old felt covered bottle hanging in the shade. Soaked with water it's well chilled by the breeze. Well Cool.

Not an endless supply of wildlife but that's not what the park is known for. It's dubbed the Cradle of Mankind. All to do with the 2 million year old skulls and skeletons found on the lakeside. A few archaeological digs and the likes. But the trail was pretty cool. Well hot and sweaty if I'm honest but I remind myself this is Africa.

We eventually make our way to Koobi Fora one of those archaeological sites on the lakeshore with a small museum chalets and camping. Just wanted the clean water and to see what was there.

Pretty rundown accommodation with only one guy holding the fort as everyone else was off on Christmas leave. Arnold had the shortest service so last one in gets to work Christmas.

He gave us two bottles of water. One chilled the other frozen. You don't know how much you miss and take things like a cold drink of clean water for granted until it's not available. I think I spent the next couple of hours topping up the partial frozen one and drinking from it as soon as the water was chilled. Don't think I even needed to pee!

Think he was glad of the company. Showed us the skull replicas and chatted about his job and family for a while. He was obviously missing home, outside of Nairobi. He let slip it was his birthday the following day. Looked quite sorry for himself. If you've ever had to work away from home for Christmas, you'll probably know that look.

He left us to a swim in the lake. Something people had been laughing about for a while when we said we were coming to Turkana. The biggest concentration of crocs in Africa apparently. You off for swim in the lake they'd laugh.

Well this stretch was clear but for a few hippos. Hey! if there was hippos there's not crocs. The hippos were far enough away not to bother us. It kinda just felt right.

[Video No. 37: **Don't Swim in the Lake**]

We had great swim together followed by a great shower. The facilities weren't the best but it's great to feel clean for a while. Dinner and watch the sun go down. Does it get much better... I'm beginning to think not...

Heading north to Ileret

We scrape out Happy Birthday in the sand before we leave camp in the morning. I'm not sure if it'll make our host any less home sick but we think it's the thing to do.

Sad to be leaving the lake-side but off we go through the rest of the park following the vaguely marked tracks. We had to turn around a few times, as we followed the same mistakes as other before us.

Dead cattle carcasses along the way were a stark reminder to us of how inhospitable this place could be.

Across the old airstrip and follow the not so well trodden trail.

Big cat tracks along the trail made you wonder what lived out here to hunt but we didn't see much. Not in the heat of the day that's for sure.

We did run into a few herders along the way. All of them running from the trail, scattering into the bush when they hear the bikes. They're not supposed to graze their animals in the park but when there is drought, needs must I suppose. The fine balance of conservation and survival. It's always them who have least who have to give up the most.

Ileret came pretty fast to be sure. The border town on the Kenyan side. A string of the Hyde covered Gadgees before a few more block-built buildings that we were used to. The locals are all friendly.

Pointing out the police station and informing us we have to go. So we did. A quick check of the passport and few details and off to the local shop for a Coke.

Thought that was it until the military looking dude waved us over.

The same routine as around the corner and we told him the police had already taken our details. The mouthy one was about to walk away with our passports when Heidi grabbed them. He let go thankfully. I was, as was Heidi feeling the shakedown coming our way. You can't respect any official trying to conduct an interview while his beer is on the table.

He was trying to tell us about the state of emergency in Ethiopia. It's not safe! The last time they had gone to Omerate across the border they had been arrested and locked up. Hey! if you didn't have a visa mate.

I told him mine was approved by the Ethiopian Ambassador himself back in Nairobi. We'd already been stamped out by the Kenyan Embassy so we'd be fine. Stood up and shook his hand. Ignored the mouthy one and walked before they could say anything else.

Turn back! Bugga that…

Met a few locals in No-Mans-Land when we stopped to enjoy our Coke. All good. Shared a few words and our Coke and moved on.

[Video No. 38: **Immigration**]

Off to the border. Unmanned we thought and a definite 1st for me.

We did find a piece of string across the track. Tied between to wooden outhouses at the edge of the village on the Ethiopian side. The locals there asked if we had a passport and when we got them out they just lifted the string and waved us on. Strange? Yeah! Different? Hell Yeah! Experienced a border crossing like it? Hell no, but we were in!

Followed the trail for a bit trying to find a place to camp. Moved on a few times as it's goat herder country. They're everywhere… But eventually we turned off the trail.

Peace and quiet in our stealth camping spot. Well, it lasted about an hour before goat boy comes walking through with AK47 on his shoulder. More a status thing than threatening. He collected the goats along with his younger brother and maybe father or grandfather. Exchanged a few handshake and we were left to it. A night in the bush listening to the hyenas and jackals. Weird Dreams! Not sure Heidi really appreciates my nightmares. More to do with the AK wheedling locals than the jackals.

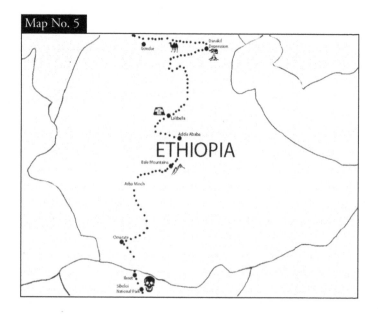

Map No. 5

25

Human Zoo

55km from the border to Omerate and the nearest police station to check in. More dusty trail but some of the poorest people I've seen in Africa thus far. Shit! They've not got much around here and I feel quite guilty for my wealth of positions.

We bounce out onto the main road and a pleasant surprise. Tarmac. And an admission from the two of us that were not sure which side we should ride on.

[Video No. 39: **Tarmac**]

We go for the right after an Italian influence in country. It proves to be right but we had to think about it for a bit.

The town of Omerate came soon enough. Police check. Immigration check customs check. Even done a bit of money changing at immigration. A kinda one stop shop…

Time for chi and something to eat before hitting the road.

Mango Camp and our tent in the shade. What a cool place. Welcomed and great to meet some English speaking friendly faces. NGO's helping out in the Hamar Community. A wealth of information on all things Ethiopian. Good company too. We left there with a list of dos and don'ts. It was a good place to start.

Into town for fuel and food. Had a quick look at the market. Busy but not that interesting. We did go to the tourist hotel for lunch and see for ourselves what the NGOs were on about. Human Zoo

Tourists… The Sandal and Sock Brigade.

Affluent tourists picking and choosing which of the locals they want in their photos. The good looking ones obviously. All the locals still in Local Hamar Drab probably does make a good picture but just seems wrong to me. Everyone paid to pose for the camera. Weird just weird.

Omo Valley

Uphill and down dale as we head east over the mountains. The kids doing some sort of strange dance at the side of the road for you. Strange form of busking me thinks. Made me laugh for their ingenuity. Excellent.

More Uphill and more down dale. Heat building and an endless stream of kids by the roadside doing their dance of hope as we go. Well, until there's one with his AK47 aimed at me. Not the first AK I've had pointed at me over the years but this one is not in anger. Not sure of what version but I am sure for some reason that he's not gonna shoot me. I watch my mirrors to see what Heidi does. Not much maybe she didn't see it so we carry on up the hill.

A decent enough road which corkscrewed its way to Konzo before turning north. A small town but supplies and a cheap hotel for the night. Beer and Tibs. We did get offered The Qat or Chat as it sounds. A leaf that you eat. A kinda stimulant. No thanks if I end up looking like you with those bloodshot eyes.

Up early the next day and out of town. That's when I first noticed how much of the Chat stuff is around. They're all at it. Even the kids… Mmm…

Off down the road enjoying the scenery when I see the cyclists in front of me. You you you Money money money I call from behind them. They turn and laugh. Monica and Rob from Switzerland. They had been on the road forever it seemed but they had focus on getting back to Europe so we're heading north at pace for them. 50-80km a day. Good going in this terrain. Told them where we were heading for the night and cracked on.

Arba Minch

The road had a sting in the tail that day and I was glad Jack Sparrow is not a pushbike.

Stopped at a band playing on a portable stage at the side of the road. Must have been a hundred revellers. A wedding me thinks. You don't stop for long before the chants of You you you, Money money money are ringing in your ears. The girls were over and Heidi's buying mangos. The crowd getting bigger and covering the width of the road. Fat bloke trying to take Heidis money. "I'm hungry" Heidi laughs and points at his paunch of a belly. Yeah you're not hungry!

I crank up the bike and just drive slowly at him. The parting of the waves and we move on. Nipped his toes with my front wheel. I offer up a fist bump and he lets out a smile as our knuckles clash. Chancer!

Arba Minch and a cool pension with safe parking. Real coffee real cold beer and a pizzeria around the corner. Run by a real Italian. Well, on his mother's side. Heaven.

The cyclists catch up and good company for a couple of nights. Never go eating with cyclists though. They'll eat you out of hoose and hame. Healthy appetites but good company.

The cyclists left early and we took the usual amount of time for our morning rituals of packing the bikes. Then we struggled to get a fuel station with electricity. Running around from station to station which were jam-packed with every Tuk-Tuk in town that had ran out of fuel. It was nearly midday before we caught up. We suggested a Coke stop at the next village and we went on ahead.

The bikes always bring attention from any kids but they turned out in their droves at this stop. Not helped by the changes of class half way through the day, so the crowd was a healthy size within mins. By the time Monica and Rob arrives there was a real spiral in the crescendo of You you you. Money money money.

No peace for the wicked it seems!

The cafe owners did their best to chase the kids, but throwing water at them but only got rocks thrown back. Rob did his best to egg them on by teasing the kids. Would have been funny on any other day but this was getting out of control.

Time to leave and a welcome relief for the cafe owners. But just one last rock from the kids which hits her on the leg and off she goes chasing them down the street. Time for a sharper exit.

Goodbyes to the cyclist as they were traveling a bit slower than us and a different route. Hey! maybe further down the road.

We crack on and enjoy the peace of the road once more. Stopping for photos only when we wouldn't be mugged by the crowds.

YouYouYou

Guba a small town and market Day. Oh! The crowd swelled all over the road. You you you Money money money ringing in my ears.

Left outside whilst Heidi checked out the guesthouse come bar. My mind was made up before she came back. No Chance! We're moving on.

This is exactly the sort of crowd you should avoid. Not a mob but hey! things can change at the drop of a hat. Remember there is still a State of Emergency.

A stark reminder as we pass a couple of burnt out trucks from the last protests just down the road.

Getting dark now and need to get off the road. But where?

Heidi asks a guy sitting on the riverbank with his family as it looked. No problem you can stay in my compound. Mohammed and his family were brilliant. They listened to our story and he would translate to those who didn't speak English. The last hour of twilight passed in no time. He suggested we wait till it was fully dark to put up the tent. He knew the score. His family helping him to his feet. Mmm... He had just gone through hip replacement surgery some six days before. He's still a young man. A good man too.

Noodles in the dark with the kids. They were no trouble, just too tired to entertain them. A peaceful night but up in the morning and a chat with them all. All interested in our sleeping arrangements and strange looking possessions. Photo session and farewells. Nice family...

Shashamane was on the main route running north south through the country. It didn't have the best of write ups in the travel guide, in fact quite the opposite to be honest. Constantly slated for poor lodgings. Glad we didn't stay, but it did give us fuel and a resupply. Good breakfast too. Food!:-) Spiced lentil dish me thinks with avocado and flat bread. The 1st time I noticed the grass / come leaves on the cafe floor. Didn't know what it was for. We guessed it would give off a fresh scent when walked upon. The burning of incense too, between that and the traditional coffee routine I was beginning to like the cafe culture here.

26

Bale Mountains

We were off to Dodola and going hiking for a few days, looking forward to getting off the bike. A great road and easy riding, the kids were good too.

The scenery was changing as we went, more mountainous for a start with an abundance of the tall growing Cyprus trees along the roadside. Just a pity Dodola was such a disappointment. It was not for long though. Into the cheap hotel and off in search of a guide to go hiking. That didn't take long either as the guiding association was close by and well organised. Be at your hotel for 02:30 ready to go. Eh? Oh! Ethiopian time 08:30 in the morning. You've got to confirm these timings. I'll get it wrong one day. The day starts at Six o'clock here.

Town was full of more military presence. Not hard targeting through the street but a show of presence. The hotel was full of them, the streets were full of them. Trying to mingle and be friends but there is an underlying distrust of them. You can see it in the locals gaze. To be honest, they who do business with them probably hide that gaze better but it's not for me to judge.

Sure enough the guys from the trekking office were there early in the morning and introductions to our guide for the next 4 days. We weren't gonna eat breakfast in the hotel but Ayano the guide had already ordered so we did too.

Nothing wrong with the food in the hotel if I'm honest. More to do with the way we're treated. Faranji Price! White tourist get a different menu and price list. If it was in the U.K. They'd be shut down for discrimination but they get away with it. You're white so we're allowed to rip you off!

Out came the table cloth which we really didn't want. All it did was draw attention to us. What a nonsense, but it seemed to justify them ripping us off. Ayano looked at me and we all looked at each other. Everyone felt uncomfortable. Was glad to get out of there. The unfortunate thing was we knew we had to go back in a couple of days. Out of town with the usual You you you. Cursed by a few for not parting with any money I'm sure. If Ayano knew what they all were shouting he didn't really let on. He seemed embarrassed by his fellow countrymen. Proclaiming they don't understand.

I'm sure something is lost in translation but you do feel uncomfortable about it all.

I did say to myself way back that I'm not getting my wallet out for anyone and I'm certainly not encouraging any kid to become a beggar. More for the personal safety thing really. It plays on your mind though and you do feel guilty.

Hiking, and I've paid for the privilege whilst putting something into the community. All the huts we'd be staying in were community run and they'd be grateful of our business. We paid more than in town even without the faranji price structure but we don't mind that. Just don't fully understand the Money money money thing.

We strode out of town and the hustle and bustle faded into the background. Streams of people did pass us from the other direction going to market. I'm sure it was probably the only time some of these folk would go into town. Supplies, gossip and catch up with old friends. Not an easy way of life but it seemed to be a flourishing countryside.

Onward and upward, continuously stopping for what seemed the endless photo shoot. I think we were both feeling the fitness thing. Or maybe the road food waistline we had acquired through Eastern Africa.

It was good to be out on the Hill… something we had both missed of late.

The mountain huts were more than just huts but basically the same design at all locations. Stick mud and brick construction with a wriggly tin roof. Comfortable inside with its own log burner. Bunk beds mattresses blankets sheet, well cozy. All your cooking utensils, stove, water purifier. Even a bottle of Coke if you wanted. Not even Faranji price! Just enough after a day on the hill. The usual noodles and whatever veg we could find. Garlic and onion essential. Magic if you can do it Chinese style. Well soya sauce if you must...

The owner came and chatted to our guide. It seemed to go on forever but hey! he was probably catching up on the news and gossip. He won't get to town that often me thinks.

The log burner didn't work but the owners son did build us a fire in one of the out-houses. An unfinished affair with no windows or doors. It let the smoke escape and it was warm but cool to sit and chat at the side of the fire. Even if you had to dodge the animal dung inside.

Awoke in the morning with more than one itchy bite around my body. Couldn't have been the hut, it was spotless. Bugga was it the out-house complete with the cow-pat minefield. It could even have been from the flea-pit hotel back in town. Who knows but bitten we were.

It could have been worse. I can still remember the good old days and the flea infestation of my past... definitely not as bad as that...

Down the other side of the mountain and another market Day in the the next village. Maybe it's a constant roundabout of market days and catch ups for the locals. Market Day in a different town/village every other day. I start thinking of home once more. Being on the hills does it to me. The most prominent thing from my Scottish heritage.

When chapman Billies leave the streets
And drouthy neebors neebors meet
As market-days are wearing late
An folk begin to tak the gate

Yip! Burns flows through my mind as I walk. I wish I was more of a scholar. Maybe one day...

The market isn't that big really but enough of what we want and a look see. Chi and dabo bread with the locals before we move on. Not before the now traditional cursing by the devil for not giving money. Hey what's new. I'm just a bad person it seems...

The scenery is pretty cool and the photo sessions continue. More out of happy snappy than needing a rest which is good. It doesn't take long to get your yomping legs back.

An earlier finish to the day and a chance of a bucket shower. Early before the sun goes down and the temperature drops. Must be almost zero at night.

Nunchucka Circus. It's has become my thing and it's what I do.

Strange music in the distance and I just presume it's the local village boom box. But no, Ayano assures me it's the local mosquey. A new one on me but then I remembered the strange music back in Konzo. They just do it differently here. It was far enough away not to make any difference. Perhaps added to that sunset moment.

Up and at it once more. A bit more of a challenge today but we're up for it. Just not into crossing the building site. A new road being driven up the valley. More progress but this one not being built by the Chinese rather an Ethiopian construction.

Good on them. Or maybe there just isn't the natural resource of ivory or diamonds to steal for the Chinese to be interested here. Whatever, time will tell if it outlasts the Chinese road building efforts.

We did find fresh bread at the construction site cafe so not all bad.

We were treated to more Beauty as we climbed. A bit of a struggle to be fair but an inward giggle as I could see our guide struggle. Amazing what will lift your spirits, as for the first time in a while I was feeling stronger. Maybe not that unfit after all.

The high point and the last mountain hut. Just in time as the heavens opened up. I had enough reminders of home thank you very much. But it did give me time to think of here. The locals way of life and the change that has gone on over the years and to come when the road is complete. Progress stops for no man…

Ayano had told us of many changes over the last few days. He probably told us more than most would tell us. At least not in public. The walls have ears and there is still a state of emergency declaration here.

Thunder Box

Not good in the morning. As if the itching wasn't bad enough I was in for my first African bad crapper day. I'd been loose before shall we say but this time I couldn't leave the long drop. Even Ayano had the dog. Feeling terrible really but we can't stay here. Push on and have the handy andys at the ready. Down the hillside without incident thankfully.

More and more agriculture on the flat lands below. Even several combines on the go. Loads of people watch while one man does all the work. Still a new phenomenon combine harvesters here me thinks. I'm sure it wouldn't draw the same crowd at home.

Into town for a Coke and catch a bus to Dodola. Minibus style. Hey! it goes when it's full. But we didn't have to wait long. Three to a double seat and a wooden mushroom stool to sit on in the aisle. The conductor looks at me to move over to let 3 on the seat. No chance if you're gonna charge me Faranji Price! I'll keep my seat I've paid for it. You're not getting it both ways. The lady still gotta seat don't worry. Just not beside me. But the bus was filled up quicker. I think he got the message. Hey! A dirty look translates in any language.

It didn't take too long but back to the Bale Mountain Hotel and more of the same treatment. Said our goodbyes to Ayano and reminded him of the conversation about home stay for other travellers like us. I'd much prefer to give him my money than the shyster in this hotel.

We'd be glad to move on from the faranji hell we'd had no choice but to buy into.

Dinsho – Bale Mountain HQ

Stunning ride up the mountain switchbacks. Endless photos shoot and video running most of the way. We reached the top of the pass and stopped to take our Happy Snappies. We did see a young girl stop in her track as she saw us. Just down the road a bit. High up on the bank she was. Never thought anything of it until the hand goes up to chuck a stone at us. My hand was already up and waving by this as I pass bye. I'm not sure if she was just a bad aim or chose not to throw at the last minute but nothing hit me.

We had read so much about the stone throwers from other Overlanders stories. Been dreading it to be honest. Even heard a conversation of some cyclist who was killed from the rock catching him on the head (not sure if this is actually true). But this was our first! Mmm… When you read the reports of the protests that sparked the latest State of Emergency. They state an American tourist died after being struck on the head by a rock. Thrown from an angry mob. Mmm… try not to think about it. It wasn't here.

Up on the plateau was awesome. A stunning winding ribbon of the black stuff. The wildlife was back, in the shape of warthogs and antelope galore. Well much more than down blow. A strange sight seeing them down on their knees grazing away. Head down arse up always helps.

Densho lodge was pretty cool but as usual we camp outside. Warthogs and all!:-)

Arranged a horse riding trip across the grasslands for the morning, a beer and chat with the other guests. Bird spotters and overland bussers. Yip! I did remember what I said about not staying anywhere there was an overland bus but they were a cool lot and we were far enough away from their bus. Good chat and a few beers before heading for the chilly night in the tent.

Bloody cold night as it turns out, and the tent's like cardboard in the morning. Hey the sun comes up and with a cuppa all is good with the World.

Great to be back in the saddle once more and I hadn't forgotten all my cowboy skills. A great way to see the grasslands.

Wild dogs shredding a goat as we leave town startles our guides horse but thankfully mine is unaffected. Yeah survival! Not sure I would have the control skills for that one. But not long till we're on our own. Well almost.

Market Day once more, and there's more people going the other way which is fine until the narrow wooden bridge across the river. But first Heidis horse goes a bit lame as she dismounts. Bloody big nail in the frog of his hoof. Could only have just happened as he couldn't have suffered that one.

Our Guide is useless at this. Just as well Heidis had horses most of her days. Lifting his hoof she's managed to ease out the nail and keep the horse calm at the same time. Walk him around a bit and he's fine. Lucky we dismounted for the bridge when we did.

Negotiate the single file traffic of the bridge and off we go. The time flew bye as we walked, come on try a canter over the grasslands. They even had me at the gallop. But it wasn't a pretty sight. I know I'm still a novice really but I'm getting there.

[Video No. 40: **Hoofin It**]

Wildlife

Back at the lodge for beer and more friendly chat. They're an older mixed group on the tour bus and for a change we actually like them. Not the students gap year party bus. Easy to chat to and valuable info for the Zanetti plateau in the days to come. Their tour guide passing on some names of fixers for the Egyptian border. Mmm... might be handy as we get closer to that day. Were both talking as if that's the natural route for us... Kinda glad the route through Turkey to Europe doesn't seem to be open.

Wolfe

First a trip up the Orimo Valley. A great biking day. Off up the trail with no kit. We don't get that opportunity often so grab it with both hands.

Friendly locals. No chants of You you you. Just Highland! The local spring water company. They're not thirsty but rather just an angle to get something. A few kids did help us find a very disappearing track so they got a share of our biscuits. Only fair. I'm not a cash machine, but they were good kids.

It was great to escape up the track and a chance to enjoy the scenery on our own. A peaceful spot for lunch by the river and time to enjoy it. You need to grab your moments in Ethiopia as you just don't know when you'll get another. We enjoyed every one of them.

Back down the valley and pick up the kit for a ride to Robe. It's not far but more convenient for the following days. Cheap hotel with a quality shower. Just what we needed. We're not disappointed.

Great ride over the Zanetti Plateau the fallowing day in search of the Ethiopian Wolf. Stunning road across the top of the plateau but at over 4000M it was mighty cold. Breath taking in more ways than one.

A chat with the radio mast keeper up top. More of a friendly photo session, but cool none the less before reaching the village on the other side. Coffee with the locals before retracing our steps. Or tyre tracks.

Rare as rocking horse sh.. apparently. No wolf for us we fear. Best time to see them out and about is early morning and not much joy for us with midday fast approaching. Just unlucky or was it the thump of the Serow? Wildlife never like the sound of the bikes. Strange to them and they'll stay clear.

I'd just about given up when Heidi stopped and got out her camera. I hadn't even noticed to be honest. Had to turn it around to see what she was investigating. Sure enough when I got my monocular out there he was. He was on edge a bit I thought, and about to do a runner at one point but he settled down once we did.

The great white hunter ghosted back down the track trying to come around him whilst I had the video camera on full zoom. Some good shots but I'd be envious of Stalkers if she got nearer. Something spooked him and they were about to pass each other by. A truck comes down the road and he's gone to ground. The last we see of him but hey! a nice encounter.

Heidi comes back out of breath and all excited. Where'd he go? But I had no answer for her. He had a bit of a limp Heidi try's to say. I had noticed and it's maybe the reason we had seen him. Out hunting longer than the rest of his kind to make up for his limp. None the less a great encounter.

Back to Robe and the hot shower. Burger beer and a warm bed. oh the simple things in life…

Online

Time for Internet cafe in the morning to try and sort out a Christmas prezzie for my daughter Lauren. Internet and 3G have been terrible since crossing the border. The governments state of emergency measures. Failure. But a begging email to Heidis dad might help. The expert shopper has all the details and it's up to him. He won't let me down. Bad fathers don't organise Christmas in time.

We're taking the non-tourist route to Addis Ababa. Via Shek Humanie. Crapy round surface rocks and bumps forever it seemed. It's relentless. Never gonna change till we hit the other side 3-400 km of it me thinks. The scenery not even that interesting. But the first of three canyons are in sight. Time for a break.

Sat at the edge looking over, we were suitably impressed. A young local woman and her kid maybe brother, come over. A chat about nothing and a share of our colo. A kinda roasted seed thing. Nice times but we must move on.

Endless dirt road does get better and more enjoyable. Must have as the GoPro cameras both run out of power!

A night tucked away in the bush. Never gonna be easy when every inch of the countryside is farmed and used for something it seemed. We're discovered a couple of times and move on. Darkness is falling and its last chance saloon but we're off the road unseen. A quiet night as we want to keep it like that. There's no troubles even if we do hear sporadic road traffic for a few hours.

Up and at it. The ride to the mosque was good enough but no peace at the village. The kids are just too excitable. Not much happens around here but we can't stay as the crowds are growing around us. I just wish we didn't attract so much attention. It seemed wherever we go it's the same. Just a pity.

Confusion reigns once more, as one of the village elders comes over and the interrogation begins. He's only trying to help but leads us off in the direction of the only Guesthouse in town. Felt like we were being run out of town if I'm honest.

We stopped him once more and ask him what's going on? Better explanation this time as we really didn't need the guesthouse. Yes a cafe for boona or chi would be good.

Quick cuppa as the kids are climbing all over the bikes and we're out of town. It's been the way of things lately. No peace for the wicked!

More canyons and switchbacks, the road's fantastic and peace once more. Could ride these trails for a while. Little settlements and small villages. Pastoralist and herders. This is the countryside that's for sure. I knew I had to stop at one point and literally had to let hundreds of cows go by. Great chatting to the herders. A whole family group I thought. At least 20 of them so you can imagine how many cows. Yip! Cow Central. Never seen this many for a while. Get the picture? Loads.

All good chat, well as much as I can make myself understood.

Another night in the bush. Just as hard to get off the road but we do manage. Eventually. Dodging the stick poking spoke bandits. WTF. Out of nowhere it seems but all of a sudden he's there in the middle of the track standing like a statue with stick in hand. He didn't move until the last minute and just threw his stick at Heidis rear wheel. Little Darling eh.

Peaceful night under the stars was in order. I for one, was surprised we got one. Missed by every goat herder around. It's our lucky day.

More of the same in the morning. The dirt track goes on and on but we can see in the distance where the main road might be. We've been at it all day and the end is just around the bend. Well almost.

We hit the road only to find the world biggest traffic jam. All trucks. Must have been 5km of them. Up the outside to the front. All sorts of hand gestures. Think they want us to turn around. Eh No!

Heidi goes to investigate and by the time she comes back I've been informed it's illegal to cross the bridge and this is some sort of security check.

Heidis lost it and giving them all what for. The boss can't or won't help. I tell him I'll have to call the embassy if he continues to treat us this way. He's just about to get on the radio hopefully to sort something out. I don't know escort or something when we get an offer from a guy with a pick up. I never even said yes and the boss has re-holstered the radio and his crew has us on the truck. Hey just go with it. How this made it safer for us I don't know. Bikes baggage with us on top all in the back of the pick-up.

No pictures! No pictures! Yeah! Yeah! we get it. Good girl! I can see the steam coming out her ears. Cock!..

Hey the bridge to Awash was a gift from the people of Japan to help elevate congestion on the old bridge on this route from the coast to Addis. Mmm… Apparently the security threat is so high and bikers aren't allowed to use it. The security checks on the truck traffic has made the congestion even worse. African logic eh…

[Video No. 41: **It's Illegal**]

I film the bridge anyway and don't understand WTF has gone on. We get dropped off in town. Reversed up to an embankment and roll them off.

The drivers mate. You must pay. You must pay. I'd had every intention of giving something for his troubles. Enough for a few beers at least. Not the 500birr he was demanding. It was a 5 min journey and there was no mention of payment back at the bridge. Hey! there's never a free lunch.

The 500birr he was demanding was for his dirty jeans. Not from our bikes Heidi told him. They were probably dirty before you started. We offer the 100birr once more to the driver. He's checking out Heidis purse and there's not much more in there. No no it's ok. But dirty jeans boys getting shirty with Heidi. He'll never know how close he came. I was about to release one in his direction. Twat... not on my watch...

The driver says give him the 15birr it will take to clean his jeans. I gave him the 100birr note and said you give him it if you must, as he's just about to get something else. Tosser...

Off to the Buffet. An old railway station converted into a guest house. Apparently Charles de Gaul and Haile Salassie have stayed here back in the good old days. In its Hay Day maybe. But it still had some character and at least the pickup boys weren't here but the thought did cross our minds. Thinking back to them asking all their question of where we were gonna stay. Nunckucka Circus flows through my head...

A great nights sleep we must say. Enjoyed the old colonial style building and its food. Well cool. It's off to Addis Ababa.

27

The road to Addis

A welcome sight but it's never easy entering the big city after being out in the sticks for so long. In my mind they all drive like maniacs. Ok, not all of them but I begin to dread these days. Trying to adjust to the flow or no flow in some cases. It's not as bad as Kampala or Nairobi for that matter but it's bad enough for the new kids on the block. Dodge, weave, brake, kick the car door I soon get back into the swing of things.

Was glad to get to the hotel though. Always more expensive in the city but this one was worth it. Clean hot shower, Wi-Fi in our room and in a good central location. Christmas is coming and we have enough admin around town to keep us busy.

Visa stuff at the embassies of Egypt and Sudan. Meet with Bisrat the guy from ETT Ethiopian Travel & Tour company for our trip to the Danikal Depression. Track down some Comesa bike insurance. Visit Ce-Lucy and some general shopping for... eh crap...

We did meet up with Joan a friend of a friend who lived in Addis. She was more than happy to give us the low down on the city.

The old time Tattoo Hotel. Rundown but still cool. Met up with a couple of Belgian bikers on their way north. Exchange of info, always good.

We had been to the Egyptian embassy a few days before and we were on our way to collect our visa hopefully. A three day turn around seemed long but they had everything in order. Swift, visit that is not the three day turn around so still time left to hit the Sudanese embassy before it closed.

The lady at the desk helped us fill in the form and we were told to come back tomorrow. Awesome how slick is that!:-) business all done before Christmas.

Collection. Oops our 30 days start running now! Not good as we wanted to tour Ethiopia first. We wanted it to start when we crossed the border. You'll have to reapply. Mmm… not us, it was your mistake. The drawback from the helpful lady filling in the forms. Bugga.

Waited 3-1/2 hours for the consular. Your fault, just reapply and pay again? No! Your fault not ours.

But But! No reasoning with this one it seems.

Get out! Get out!

I think I've been thrown out of better places but it would have been my first embassy ejection. He did calm down and eventually told us to come back 21st next month and he'll extend it… Reluctantly… but hey! what can you do. Maybe the 3 day turn around at the Egyptian Embassy wasn't that bad after all.

Christmas is a bit unorthodox or is it? Orthodox Christmas is the 7th January.

Wow! no Santa and no celebrations so we opted for the now only traditional thing that's left. The Indian meal. Expensive but hey! we had no prezzies apart from Toblerone and a bottle of wine. Just glad Heidis dad had sorted out my gift to Lauren.

There was enough around town to entertain us. A trip to the museum and an English language cinema. Rogue 1. Pizzerias burgers bars and pastry shops. All with the professional beggars outside. Its a life long trade, especially when your brought up with it. I find it hard to take when the kids are taught their trade from such an early age.

Whole families siting outside the bakery proclaiming they're hungry but all orchestrated by the father from 30 yards down the road. Money for his habits I'll bet or is that just me being cynical.

Worse than that was the two attempts of pick pocketing on me. Both with the same trick.

Boy walks in front of me with a flash magazine held out between us as if for sale. Another comes up the other side and grabs my arm asking for money. Whilst your distracted the hand under the magazine is trying your pocket.

This is not your lucky day! I grabbed the hand down through the magazine twisting his arm up his back and threw him against the wall. Unfortunately there's a beggar sitting right there in the street. He falls over the beggar. Maybe it is his lucky day as if he hadn't fell over the beggar I might just have pounded him against the wall a bit more. A few verbal outburst by me and everyone around looking in our direct knows what's gone on. Hey! only a few yards and a 4x4 stops, rolls down the window. You ok? I'm in contact with the police and holds up a radio.

No I'm fine. No need to explain really as he's seen it all.

The very next day the same trick is forming around me. This time I turn and startle the distraction and he doesn't fancy the clenched fist that's formed in front of him and backs off. The mag lad is a bit more persistent but he to realises it's not gonna be his day and runs. A guy getting out of a local mini bus seen it and was now shouting down the street at them but the guy in the Peugeot forecourt has only seen me threaten a couple of youths. A bit of finger wagging going on.

You want your city known for thieves and pick pockets? No I think not! As he soon realises the situation and let's it go. Can't believe he had thought to have a go at me... Rogue 1 was cool and settled me down. I'm at one with the force. A few beers helped me too.

FaceTime with those who matter most. Nanny, mum & dad and Lauren. Well worth being in the city. But as usual it's always nice to leave. Not before a bit of money changing but that doesn't take long. Let's get out of here.

Lalibela

700ish kilometres so not in one go. Out of town, the ride was good enough and good enough tarmac all the way to show a rabbit. Not how you spell it but how you say it. So a bit of a shock to find a couple of broken spokes on Heidis rear wheel. The penny drops and the little fooker throwing a stick at the spokes on the way to Awash. Another little trick of the Ethiopian brats at the side of the road.

We took out the broken ones and got the oil change finished. Worry about it in the morrow.

Jimmy the floors wet! Jimmy the floors wet!

Half asleep I stand up out of bed to find the room floor an inch deep in water. Oh Dear!

We get one of the cleaners. Much panic and she picks up the duvet as we pick up our belongings off the floor. She exits and we sit on the bed. Mmm...

Nothing for ages so we go get the manager and he's no clue. She never said.

Bugga this let's just pack and go.

All packed and sitting waiting on the manager to say something. Broken water pump. What about all our clothes? There soaking!

He shrugs his shoulders. Sorry! With a school boy grin. Twat...

Coffee out on the street and we ask a biker about spare spokes. He takes us to a bicycle shop. No spokes. There's a mechanic down the street. Come come. My heads down but goes along with it still fearing the wild goose chase around town. Two mins later out comes the mechanic with a bag of Yamaha spokes. Result!:-) There not exact, but close enough.

Coffee with bread and honey. What a start to the day.

We crack on checking the rear wheel as we go. Spraying the spokes with WD40 for what's to come. Heading for the lake and hopefully a secure campsite to change out the spokes. Can't stop thinking about the stick in the spoke gage. Little Fookers

Can't stop thinking about the flooded hotel room. A did crack a smile as I stop for pee and find last nights hotel room key in my pocket. Oops. Over the side for you. I hoped the door was locked when they eventually went to clean it. Twat... me probably for the childish ditching of the room key but I put it down to way we been treated lately.

No camping but a bamboo Rondavaal. Hey! there's a compound and peace to fix the wheel. On any other day it would have been cool place. Thank Fook for WD. With a bit of persuasion the spokes are in place. Not perfect but they'll have to do.

Slept much better for it.

Up the China road towards Lalibela. Really enjoyed it but me thoughts were never far away from Heidis rear. Wheel that is...

The road's full of potholes but the scenery makes up for it. The mountain switchbacks are a bikers heaven. What a ride. Well until we hit the construction site. I lost count of how many kilometres we rode through the building of the new road. Relentless it just went on and on. Long day in the saddle and almost dark when we got to Lalibela. Easy decision at the hotel and a good one too. The room far better than we had expected. Well at least we're not gonna be flooded out... we hope...

Museum first and then the churches. 13 monolithic masterpieces. My ramblings won't do them justice. I'm genuinely in awe as we walk around the site. Bemused of how they built them back in the day. Fantastic as they're still in use by the locals too.

No guide for us as we like to meander at our own pace but we've read and know enough to work a lot of it out. I can't get hung up to much on the historical facts of the place but you can't fail to be impressed.

Freedom to roam and going against the tide sometimes, we spent the best part of two days checking out the site.

Nooks & Crannies.

China Road

Out of town and the China road. It's Hogmanay but there's no party to go to so we may as well ride. A dusty affair with all the pilgrims heading in the opposite direction as usual but we had made plans to go to the Danikal the day after the morrow and it's a 2 day ride. Uphill and down dale but a good road. Dirt and Gravel the way we like it but me minds never far from Heidis rear.

More hands out shouting money money money but a bit more aggressive. The stone throwing has become a regular thing. Fooker I don't understand it.

Heidis in front as I've been playing with me camera. Little git at the side of the road lobs one at her. As I come along his attention turns to me. This time his hands out for money with the rock in the other. I stop at the side of the road. Hey! all I get is the rock. Little darlings. Ok maybe not what I said, but good job he ran. Just about finished with them by now. Hit once in the heed and once in the thigh. Mmm…

We did manage to get off the road without being seen so tent in the starry night hotel.

Happy New Year…

Up and at em!. Too many foot prints and cattle tracks for it to stay quiet for long. We did get time to have our breakfast in peace and pack before the beasts of burden arrived with herder in tow. The nick o' time me thinks.

Down the road and a check of the kit. Shit another spoke has gone. Take out the broken bit and worry about it later.

Amazing how you can get stoned one day and an offer of help or a lift the following but we're fine. So carry on to Mekele

Cheap hotel and fix the spokes once more. Re pack our kit for the Danakil. We join the tour tomorrow.

The Danakil Depression

We'd been looking forward to this for a while. Probably because it's like nowhere else on this earth of ours. The salt beds lying some 125m below sea level. Averaging 100mm of rainfall per year. Hottest year round temperatures of anywhere making whatever rainfall there is evaporate oh so quickly. Hotter than hell no…

The Ce-Lucy fossil skeleton was found here. At over three million years old, a real throwback to the early beginnings on man. Maybe not the most hospitable but an intriguing place to say the least.

Stretching out over ten thousand square kilometres from the Afar Region of northern Ethiopia to Eritrea. A volatile border region for many a year. The unrest in this region sometimes described as lawless but that just might be the least of your worries.

With more than one volcano, the Erta Ale being the newest where lies an open lava lake from where you can take a look over the edge to what lies beneath. In the Dalol there are hot springs which ooze sulphuric acid stirred up from the very depth of the earth.

The Lowest, The Hottest, The Driest, not to mention sulphuric acid oozing lava lakes. Hey! It's a must see… No?

28

Un-Orthodox Christmas

ETT travel and tours. It seemed like the thing to do. A rough calculation and it would be $460 a head if we wanted to visit the Danakil. Permits security police and military. Also we would have to have hired two 4x4 to carry them around with us. Oh and their drivers. Just not practical so when we asked this tour company they said no problem just tag along. We'll do the rest. Carry our kit for the 480 km trip. Apparently it's a bit rough in places with deep sand in others so we were glad of running with no luggage for a change. Besides I'm not sure we could have worked it all out. The permit stuff I mean…

Out and meet the crew at their hotel. A slow start getting all these people together. 10 Toyota Land Cruisers with at least 4 to a car. Mmm… Takes some organising but we chatted with Devon and Steve who were on the trip. Steve the West Ham fan and Devon's a student from the States. Won't hold that against him. I'll let you work out which.

Chat about travel where you've been where you're going the usual stuff but it's all good.

Eventually we're off. We've managed to leave some stuff in the office and the gear we're taking with us is dumped in the car. Happy days. 4 of them with no kit to carry. That doesn't happen very often.

Extended slow start as we only travel 40km before our first coffee stop. Mmm…

Fish the tour organiser has his hands full so enjoy the coffee with the Italians. Good chat as they've got the Ethiopian connections. Not so much about us which we like.

Up and go, a ride through the canyons. Lower and lower with the heat rising. Lots of photo shoots which is good but arse to keep control of. Probably one of the reasons we don't do organised trips normally. Hey it is what it is.

Small town village for lunch. Pleasant enough but I'm not at ease leaving the bikes unattended. But lunch and chill out for a bit. The kids all fascinated with the helmet and cameras. Yip I know my audience.

I can see one bike from where I'm sitting but there's a lesson here. Make sure you can see both as the street kids are rifling through Heidis bar bag. Pump, puncture outfit, pills but worst of all the sun cream. Jimmy's factor 50. The Danakil is one of the hottest and most inhospitable places on earth and the little gits have nicked me factor 50. WTF do they want with that. Nothing it seems as the lady in the cafe chases them down the street, firing rocks and hurling insults as she goes. Top shout! By the time she comes back with the rest of the chasers they've picked up everything but the puncture repair kit. Little darlings eh!

Finally all the paperwork is sorted and our escorts are in place well enough for them to allow us to continue. Money talks Eh!

More of the scenic stuff but up ahead a camel caravan is just about to cross out path. Well, the road really.

Step back in time as this journey has been going on for hundreds of years. The Afar people cut the salt into blocks and load them onto the camels for the 300km journey to the road end. It's then transferred out into the countryside through a network of salt merchants. Increasing in value 10 fold along the way. This caravan was on its way back. Not quite empty as it was carrying supplies for them and the other Afar salt cutters.

What a sight. Slow but purposeful. Steady and methodical. If my camera was in black & white I really would have had travelled back in time.

Onward to the salt pans

The Afar village is at the end of the road. A ramshackle affair with no real structure. Wooden shacks with tourist tour company tents intertwined. Oh! and more kids that just don't know their boundaries. You can't leave the bikes anywhere. More Toyota land cruisers than you can throw a stick at but their fingers all over the bikes. Bugga…

Not long before we're out on the salt and peace is restored. Easy time watching the camel caravan to and fro. That timeless photo shoot watching the Afar at work whilst the sun goes down. Photo shoot heaven.

Back to the village as that's where the military post is and we have to stay. Not the best ride back in the dark as Heidis front light is still not working. But with mine on full beam and the light reflecting off the salt there was enough. No good for the video but we managed.

Starry Night Hotel. Wooden cots lined up under the stars you can't beat it.

It is a bit much that it's describe as an open toilet when there is no facilities and a thousand piles of shit surrounding the village. Mmm… Something I just can't understand…

Well no one stole anything during the night and we're up early to a good breakfast and coffee. A big day is on the cards.

Roll out across the salt and the land cruisers disappear one by one. Slippy under foot. Not even the nearly new Mitas can cope at speed here. Nice and steady but that suits us as the scenery is stunning. It wasn't long before we all closed up and parked at the start of the Dalol. A quick briefing and freedom to roam.

More spectacular colour than I've ever seen in one place. Pity about the smell as the sulfur is overwhelming at times. Splurged into the air by the little geezers blowing off steam. A steady stream of that spiralling upwards and carried away on the breeze.

Fluorescent greens yellows and red. All variations of oranges to rust like crustaceans. Truly speechless as we try to suck it all in. The tour group doing the tour group things. Posing for selfies and trying to out do each other with pics with guitars to posing with the military. Hardware on show of course!..

If I hang back a bit I eventually get to enjoy the view and take the pictures and video I want.

I had to endure the military selfie photo shoot but it took me back in time. I was no different. I've got most of those pics at home.

[Video No. 42: **Dalol Colour**]

We could have stayed longer but happily tag along as everyone heads back to the cars. It's as hot as hell!

Off to the sand cliffs and caves with a stop at the hot springs. Highly unusual scenery just seems to be the norm. More photo shoots.

But further and further out onto the salt flats we can see the Afar salt cutters at work. The camels sitting around whilst the salt blocks are extracted and cut to shape.

There's a natural flaw in the surface that's left by the drying process. It's these flaws that are used. Manipulated by axes and wooden podgers. Lifted and manhandled enabling another to shape with a shorter hand axe. A labour intensive salt block production. Up to 40kg per camel. Quite a load considering how far they have to carry it.

Me thinks health & safety back home would have a meltdown if they saw the whole process all carried out in traditional garb and Chinese jelly shoes. The safety boots of choice.

It's hotter than hell and to be honest I'm not sure I could handle a shift here.

Off once more. We've got a few kilometres to cover before tonights guesthouse. Lunch along the way but no sticky fingers this time.

Village

Ditch our kit in the guest house and follow the 4x4 land cruisers to the river. The bikes are caked in salt and it's got to come off. The land cruiser would suffer just as bad and it seems to be a Danakil tour routine. Clean it off in the river. One of the older kids takes control and we're happy to let him. A small price to pay.

Great nights rest with good food and good company. Cold beer or two to wash it down.

Finishing off a cup of coffee and fish the tour guide wants a word. We've brought the spare fuel but there is space in the car if want to leave the bikes. It's a tuff track and we don't want you to be disappointed. Mmm… putting the frighteners on me, me thinks.

It was your office that told us the wrong total of kilometres so cheers for the fuel but I'll be riding my bike. let's put it this way. I don't see much in the way of sand boards on the cars or any digging tools for that matter. We'll be fine. I don't think he was happy but just not my concern. The Crazy-one is in complete agreement when I tell her.

Easy morning but more delays and hanging around waiting for permits and security. Lunch seemed to last an eternity. Time I could have been paddling through the sand. Eventually we hit the trail, a dusty one but not as bad as we were led to believe. The bikes are handling it better than before. The god send of no kit to carry. All is good. In fact by the time we reach the lava road it doesn't take long to leave all the land cruisers behind. We may have been slightly

slower on the sand. Well, they did stop a few times but mostly for the photo shoot so we coped. Now on the lava they were a lot slower than us. Time for us to just enjoy the ride. Can't go wrong on a well-trodden trail and we reach the military camp in no time.

[Video No. 43: **Support Crew**]

Chill and sort yourself out for a bit of night yomping to the volcano.

A slow trek to start with but it shakes itself out and everyone finds their pace and place snaking up the hillside. We had to content ourselves with following those who had torches. Mmm… left ours in the tent bag back in town. Would have been better with them me thinks.

Plenty of rest stops along the way as not all are hikers or hill walkers but we do catch up with the camel train that is carrying the mats and sleeping bags. Stacked high they were and in the dark. Quite glad of the beasts to carry the kit if I'm honest.

It's after 11 when we reach the upper camp and you can see the reddish glow in the not too far distance.

Stumbling as we go making our way following the man in front the plod of your footstep turns to a crunch. The blackened waves of lava stretches out in front of us. The heat has escaped this volcanic over- flow but it's not solid. Almost meringue like in places. A hard crust with softer powder crumble underneath. Just glad there is none of the goo left behind as your feet fall through.

It's slow going with many including us stumbling in the dark. We reach the rim with oohs and ahs all round. The Danakil is hotter than hell and now we're look down into there. You can imagine auld Nic himself screeching a tune oot o his fiddle just over the edge. A mesmerising sight...

Above the buzz o chatter of the others you could hear it bubble, hiss, crackle and snap then spit up molten lava. Rarely breaching the sides but when it does reach for freedom the lava simply lands on the white rim bubble and slowly slither back down. Not all of it mind you. That reach for the the sky leaves a residue which covers the rim cooling, growing every time. The rim changing shape as it does so. There is the odd occasion when the red stuff does reach out over the rim. Shooting skyward like fireworks and coming to ground all around the Faranji tourists. Scarily none of them moving as they are so mesmerised by what's going on around them to be in fear of their safety.

A magical sight but It hadn't gone on un-noticed that we've been on the go all day and it's now one in the morning. I could have stayed a while longer but our bed was calling. Retracing our steps we stumble through the darkness once more to find the mattress that was the Starry Night Hotel.

Awesome to be under the stars once more. Eerie dreams of Tam O

Shanter... those thoughts of Auld Nic... "weel done cutty sark! and in an instant! all was dark"...

Ooh Diesel

Up before dawn and a walk up to a different vantage point for a final gaze at the lava lake. Just amazing but we had a 3 hour walk down the hill in front of us... What a plod...

Breakfast back at the base camp. What a dump. In the daylight, every bit as bad as the hovel we left up top.

Chatting to Fish the tour guide there was lots of questions about the camps. Mostly the one about the 10,000 piles of shit and no toilet. His explanation just sounded like bullshit to me. Yeah I heard it...

After being fed we slipped the leash knowing full well that by the time we reached the sand the trucks would have the legs on us.

The head start was all we needed beating half of them to the roadside. Not that enjoyable after the nights activities. Off to the salt lake for a swim and lunch before the ride back to town.

We said our farewells as we presumed it would be the last we saw of the trucks.

Thankfully not all of them disappeared into the distance as me Bike choked and stalled. There was three 4x4 that pulled alongside but if none of them were mechanics then all they were was a distraction. Good intentions but just a distraction. Urging me to drain the bad fuel out the carb. Hey! I'll let it cool and have a think. On you all go. People have planes to catch. Farewells once more.

The bike was hot as was everything. Had I cooked the bloody thing? God only knows. I let it cool down and changed the spark plug. It was white hot at the business end. Mmm... Drained the carb of any Debris. Wishing I had done these things one at a time. Hey it started and I plodded along. The guys had phoned ahead saying we had trouble but we didn't have a number to call to say we were going once more. They were on their way and we met soon enough.

No mechanic amongst them but they follow behind for a while.

The bike stopped a few times more. Only starting after cooling down. Made no sense to me, I'm no mechanic. You got a bit of rope we can borrow? They did and we started towing the Sickly JackSparrow. We had done this once before for about a kilometre back in Bulgaria. Wasn't much of a success then but that was all we needed. This time much further. Over 100km further. We soon got into the swing of things in fact got the hang of it. Well mostly! Footpeg to footpeg and the guys in the truck were amazed, even if we only wanted to travel at 40kph. We sent them on saying we'd manage.

Uphill and down dale once more with darkness falling. Not what we wanted, with Heidi no headlight and me no tale light. Mmm... We put on opposite indicators to act like hazard warning lights. We managed! It was pretty tense at times when the big trucks came buy with no headlights on. Bugger what are they thinking? Can't they see what's going on? Obviously not! Mystifies me why they do that. Saving there headlights. Or so they think. Madness.

Apparently you save on fuel when you run without your headlights on. A study in the states suggest somewhere in the region of $3 to $10 a year for the average daylight driver. Not a fortune even in Africa so why would you run without you lights on during the darkness hours.

Not what we wanted but it is what it is. We'd make the guest house with a bit of luck.

Which we did. Well after dark and exhausted. Everyone asking the same questions but we don't have the answers. If I did, believe me, I would have fixed it!

Just In time for supper and a beer. Only one though. We couldn't keep, our eyes open. Worry about it in the morning.

Morning came to soon to be honest and my prayers that it would all go away went un-answered. Up and deal with it.

If I can't get it going we're towing it into town. Empty the fuel tank. Bugga it's like a cowboy coffee sludge in the bottom of there. Not putting that back in. Clean out the bottom of the carb. Well as fair as I've been before when cleaning it. But it did look a bit oily. Clean the spark plug. Check that it sparks. It does so just about as much as I can manage for now… Turn it over and see what happens. No Joy!

[Video No. 44: **Camel Jockey**]

Checking under the tank just to make sure I hadn't shaken the spark plug suppressor cap lead loose in my efforts with the tank. Honk honk! Shit I scrape me fingers off the cylinder head as I jump back. *Bugger Off!* As my rage got the better of me. The kids all went running. Normally not bad with kids interest but did I mention these ones know NO boundaries. Unbelievable…

Hey! lets just tow it up the hill and I'll try bump start it on the run down.

It did fire up of a fashion but it just wouldn't run… Towing it to town then…

Exhausted and stressed we went back to the hotel we stayed in the last time. Heidi got the luggage from ETT office and I cracked on. Her chesty cough not getting any better from all this. Just leave me to it.

Can't believe she managed so well at the towing malarky, but she did. We were both rundown with our efforts of the last few days.

Started the whole process once more. Changed my chain and sprockets as I went. More because I didn't know what else to do. I did strip the carb that bit further. Out with the diaphragm and there's the problem I think. Full of an oily residue… No! That's feckin diesel!

My anger gets to me as I remember the guys in the truck urging me to empty the carb. They had brought the fuel can and knew what was in it before. No petrol trucks on the tour. Fookers

I calmed down and cleaned the carb as best as I could. Spotless it was. Still no joy. I wrote the whole sorry saga down and sent a message to Jim. I'm in luck it's milk time back in the U.K. Workshop. Tells me to change the plug even if it's got a spark it's not strong enough. Just washed out because of the diesel. I steel Heidis and put the jump leads on her battery and it fires straight up. WooHoo!!!

No more spare plugs and it's orthodox Christmas so we'll have to hang around for a few days before getting a new one. Oh deep joy! Sunday as well make that 4 days in all. Both Heidi and I can do with the rest, exhausted to be honest... Merry Christmas...

29
What a debacle

Axum – Simien – Gondar

It had seemed like an eternity in Mekele. Spent more days than we thought we would. The bikes yeah but we both needed to recover from some sort of dreaded lurgy. Just exhausted but we did eventually hit the road to Axum. More than a few kilometres for sure but the road is stunning. Had the video running for an age. Just Stunning! Can't believe the back drop to this crazy road trip.

Cheap Hotel and dinner in the roadside restaurant. Cool place with a laid back feel. Up to see the obelisks in the park. Check out the churches. Even had a look see at the Ark of the Covenant. Well the door that it's said to be kept behind! Museum and a coffee. Pizza for dinner. Very civilised…

[Video No. 45: **The Ark**]

What a place, well cool but the clock is ticking if we want to go hiking.

Off to Debak…

Stone throwers once more but I suppose they've never really been away. Hit in the head once more and one little fooker even had a swipe at me with a stick… Hard to fall in love with Ethiopia!

The road made up for it. Just as good as going to Axum was the road out and it continued all the way to Debak.

Another cheap hotel. This time not so cheap so we go around town to find a Cheaper pension. Breakfast included. Good deal and they would keep our luggage if we went hiking. Top shout.

Into town to find the scout association and park office. We work out a plan for 4 days and pay our fees. Wait a moment, I'll go organise a scout for you. Lots of discussion as he would have to sit on the back of the bike. Most of them were older and if they had that experience before they didn't want it again. We ended up with a younger guy. Malissa. Well, it was what it sounded like to me and he did answer to it.

Out the door and up the trail leaving town behind us. Not that comfy but we stopped at all the view points for a look see. Trip to the waterfall and back. You had to use your imagination as it's the dry season but it was impressive enough. Camp at the mountain's hut and hit the hill tomorrow after the ranger station. The bikes will be safe there.

I'm sure they would have been if we had paid the 300birr extortion money for parking. Fook That. I've just about had enough of this feckin country. Your nothing but a Thief. Feckin Twat! I'm not paying!

Heidi does her softly softly bit but he's adamant that our bikes are not safe and he'll have to guard them and wants paying.

Twice the price of our daily scout fee. 150birr. Cock!

Let's just go to Chennek and walk from there. Not giving this one nothing. So we left.

Chennek was always on the list but more for a view and a place to stay, not the start point for hiking. It takes longer than we think to get there. Late morning and we're at altitude that's for sure. The bikes been stuttering for a while. Let's just enjoy the view and take a ride up top in the afternoon.

A breath-taking place in more ways than one. Neither of us have recovered fully from the Danakil lurgy. Maybe it's best we don't go hiking. Trip up top in search of the Walya Ibex and back a day early.

We spent the next couple of hours making plans for our African exit. Hell! we had been putting it to one side but it needed talking about. We had gathered information along the way but hadn't talked in depth about it.

Plans afoot…

Up the hill in search of the Ibex. The bike really struggling now. Hey! 4000m what did I expect. Stuttered all the way in 1st mostly but it did climb it. At the top we only waited a few minutes and there he was. An absolute stunner in all his glory and in a perfect spot for his portrait. Amazing! Kinda made it all worthwhile. Happy to pay Malissa his fee just for finding the Ibex.

Easier rolling downhill with plenty stops for the photoshoot. Malissa eagerly getting involved, posing with his rifle in hand. An old Italian Carcano me thinks. I'm no gun spotter but if it is, then it is what Lee Harvey Oswald shot Kennedy with. Yeah a museum piece but here it's just a throwback from the Italian colonial days.

[Video No. 46: **Riding Shotgun**]

The long road to town was exactly that, long!

Thanked Malissa before going into the park office.

The managers not here. Please put your comments into the suggestion book. Mmm…

If there's no manager then I'll have to go to the police. Man with gun extorting money from faranji tourists in the park.

What with the current state of emergency this got her attention. Not good for business.

20sec later. Oh! the Manager.

We gave him the saga and he seems genuinely concerned about the situation. I can't give you a refund. All permit moneys go to the government. They never give back. We can give your scout fees back.

I look a Malissa but me and Heidi had already discussed this. No! I'd like to state here and now. Our scout did a great job. We're very happy. But park Ranger extorting money from tourists? Well, we've covered that. I hope you do something. He assures us he will. We actually believe his sincerity. Maybe he will.

Gondar Awaits

But hey back to the old routine. Stone Throwers. Fook! Not one whilst Malissa was on the back, at least a dozen the 1st day he's not. I'll never understand it. I'll have to get myself a gun it seemed to work for him. Maybe just a mannequin with a stick! Maybe not that realistic but come on when will it end.

Gondar comes soon enough and we find Belagez a great little pension that will keep our bikes and luggage whilst we take the bus to Addis. Sudanese visa dates are still wrong but if we can sort it out in a couple of days we can sit out our Ethiopian visa on the lakeside and relax for a change. We're still suffering from the after effects of the Danakil lurgy.

Mmm... Timkat... Ethiopias most holy days...

Took an eternity to get to Addis with holy men being paraded through every town along the way. Red carpet treatment. The one from the back quickly rolled up and rolled out in front whilst he walks along under a gazebo on wheels shading himself from the sun. Bizarre but who am I?

Bugga even the Sudanese embassy has taken the Timkat holiday and closed for four days. That's our lakeside plan up the creak...

Enjoy what Addis can offer you. Time to research our escape from Africa plans and a fantastic Indian meal. I'm sure I've mentioned this before... we deserve it.

Embassy was good to their word and re-stamped the visa. They just never said it would only be a one week extension. Bugga just not worth the effort. Let's go but wait, one more sting in the tale. Four bus companies and no seat for tomorrow. So have to wait yet another day. Hey! how many more plans do we have to make.

Back in Gondar and the people at the pension Belegez do us proud. Looked after all our gear and bikes and never asked a penny. A rarity for Ethiopia me thinks.

A look around Gondar Castle which was worth it even if we only gave ourselves a few hours. The local TV crew asked for an interview but didn't seem to film much as I talk in my best Scottish accent. Heidi just laughs… glad we can still smile.

Out to Lake Tana. Tim & Kims Village.

Quit aggressive stone throwers on the way even a stick welding road block but we're not stopping for that. It's Hard to fall in love with Ethiopia.

Lakeside and a rest. Only the 2 days. Not what we had planned but it is what it is. There are no stone throwers here. Bliss for a couple of days and plenty of chat about Ethiopia with Kim. Her advice is just don't try and understand it…

Short-sighted – Kids are left alone and un-attended till 6 or 7 – Stone throwers – Cyclist and the spoke pokers – Corruption – Tattoos to chase away the spirits – The Chat thing – Money Money Money. Not when she first came 16 years ago (Kinda don't believe her).

Kim had, but it's Hard to fall in love with Ethiopia

Put all aside for the moment as we never felt so peaceful. Really wished we could have had that time to ourselves by the lake. We could have used the chill time.

Blowing Off Steam

Is It All Just Me? It's was a relief in many ways when leaving Ethiopia. Looking forward there's No Stone Throwers for a start…

The journey up Lake Turkana was stunning. Everything I thought it would be and a whole lot more, just fab. Ethiopia on the other hand, well it was so varied. It changed every day and never stopped surprising you. It's hard to fall in love with, what with the stone throwers and all. But it was stunning. More history there than the rest of Africa. And it's real, alive and you can touch it.

Stunning scenery, beautiful backdrops, and sublime skylines. The monolithic churches of Lalibela are almost unbelievable. The truly wonderful part about it is that there still accessible and still used by

231

the pilgrims. As is most of the monuments of old. And The Danakil is not of this earth. The first steps to Hell me thinks.

But, and there always is one! Or two!

The You you you Money money money. The Stone Throwers. The stick in the Spokes Gag. The Faranji Price Structure. WTF!

There are some 96 million people in this country and more than half of them with their hand out. I know some of them don't have much but there is no one, NO ONE in this country who approaches you with just the how you doing in mind. Everyone who does has an angle to get something out of you. Unbelievable! I've never felt less charitable and most of my Christian thoughts toward my fellow man escaped me. Not a good feeling.

We've almost travelled the length of Africa and no one's stolen anything off the bikes until here. Along the way I've always watched our backs but I've been the victim of two pickpockets attempts and several non-understandable outbursts by complete freaks. Bugger being surrounded by the one hundred strong crowd chanting You you you Money money money is enough for any man and one I'll never forget. Yip! Ethiopia, its hard to fall in love with, believe me!

Map No. 6

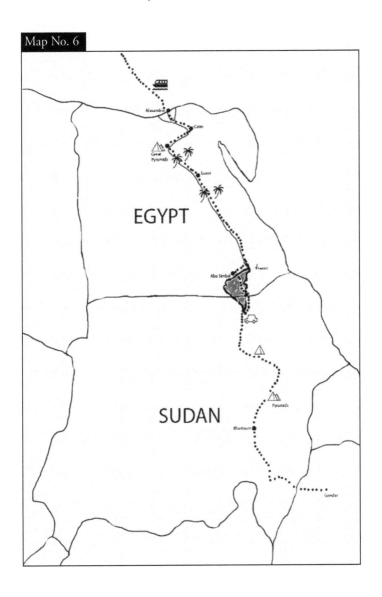

30
The Sudan

An unknown to us both. It was a stumbling block when we first thought of coming to Africa. No shipping going south from Europe to Egypt at the time and the only real passenger ferry came through Israel. No guarantee of not getting a stamp in your passport there, so a real stumbling block if you then want to enter Sudan. Other Overlanders have said in the past when they've visited Israel the authorities have put a removable paper stamp in their passport. Just not that confident that's what would have happened. Not even the unfavourable route through Turkey was available.

All in all, no great shakes while coming from Cape Town north then. Solved that one!

But we then never really looked into Sudan the country much more. It probably added to the surprise. We all know of the war and Africa's newest country in South Sudan. But after that, not much more.

The only thing was, you had to register with the authorities in Khartoum within three days of crossing the border so we had to get our heads down and ride for a change. It was ok, two full days riding and we were there. A great nights camping in the desert along the way… One of our best me thinks…

You learn nothing with your head down arse up kinda thing. Not even what the locals eat or drink. Ride and try work it out as you go.

Never the easiest when you first cross the border. You need time to tune into the local way of life.

Enjoy the desert scenery for what it gives for now.

We had no intentions of staying for long in Khartoum. When we get our paperwork done then we could escape the city and the quiet life of the desert. Not that we needed to run away but it's the way we were feeling. There was time for a visit to the national museum which gave us a great insight to what may lie ahead as we were to travel north. Oh! and the must of seeing where the Blue and white Niles meet just along the road. Not to mention the now traditional song and dance routine with the local money changers… They make some prophet and we don't get robbed…

Out looking for coffee in the morning. No cafe but a host of street venders. We got captured by a local man and an Iraqi now living in Khartoum. Great company and we couldn't pay for our coffee. Something that was to happen to us on more than one occasion through Sudan.

But escape we did. Eating like a local with chi and boona stops along the way. Mountains of foul and bread. Awesome salads and hummus-tahini

Just get out and ride… Into the desert. 30km from the road to be honest.

Deserted!

Pitch your tent and cook your noodles.

Two Minute Noodles… Entertained myself by filming the episode.

[Video No. 47: **Two minute noodle**]

No need for the tent outer and found ourselves watching the stars before drifting off to dreamland.

Gunfire

The rude awakening. Gunfire and a shake from the light sleeper but the gunfire was enough. I was bright eyed and bushy tailed.

She had been watching the search lights coming down the valley for a while. Some sort of truck with head lights on full. Search lights swivelling on their mounts.

Bugga my heart was racing. More gunshots. Time to bug out!

But as I went for my jeans the lights turned and changed direction.

We watched the lights go and then fade into the distance. Still trying to come up with an explanation for it all.

We lay there for what seemed like forever. Watching! Listening!

Drift back into dreamland only to be awoken once more but this time the gunshots were in the distance and not so alarming.

It did make for a more active dreamland.

Restless Jimmy thrashing and kicking out in sleep apparently. Barking my orders to others in the firefight I'd got myself into… not sure he's ever gonna leave… Demons never leave easily…

In the morning all was good and yip! The kids from the stick houses not so far away came around a watching the strange tourists pack up their tent.

All smiles and waves. So considering the action of the night before all I can say is it could or must be the norm. Maybe Lamping for wildlife. Whatever chases the goats and what not round here.

Yet another interesting night in the desert.

Temple Days

Only a couple of kilometres to the site of Roman kiosk of Naga. Think we woke the security Guard out of his morning ritual.

With his glass of chi in hand he looked through and kept the copy of our travel pass. Wanted $25 US each to get in. Eh! Maybe not.

If all these sites are that much to get in then we won't be seeing much of them.

No bluff but when I go to ride off he stops me and says it's ok.

He was good about it too.

It was in ruins really, but interesting enough.

The short ride to the Temple of the Lions

The same there. No one really around but then the jog across the sand towards us.

Still not paying the tourist price.

He also changed his mind as I went to ride off but charged us the local rate.

All good. It wasn't a bluff. Not skint yet but we're aware of the budget.

Bumped into an Aussie who lives in London. He was full of good chat and well-travelled. His guide was Shady, a wealth of info. We picked his brains of what lay ahead and said he would make some calls for us. He knew how expensive it was for tourist around these sites. Good guy.

Back to the road and move on. Easy riding but with only a two week transit visa maybe we should make some distance.

Merowe and the site of Begrawea came soon enough. A group of a dozen or so pyramids sitting just off the roadside.

As we turned off we got the camel jockey escort to the entrance. They were no hassle really only trying to attract some business. Unlucky lads! Not from me...

A beautiful site to be honest. Sitting up on the Sand Dunes you could imagine the grandeur of the days gone by. Peaceful and Very chilled. We had the place to ourselves. Well almost. Best thing was, Shady the guide from this morning had phoned ahead and we didn't need to ask the price. Straight away charged the local rate. Awesome. Did what he said he would.

[Video No. 48: **Pyramids**]

Sitting Chatting with the guardians was cool but we needed to find a camp spot for the night. Preferably one without gunfire.

The guardians suggested the other side of the mountain. This is Sudan no one cares where you sleep. Cool so we did.

Awesome pitch in the dunes. Soft landing for when the mattress deflates during the night.

More stick fires to cook on which isn't that easy in the desert. Well easy enough to light but not so easy to find the firewood. Something we would have to collect as we go over the days to come.

Peaceful night with a wonderful sunrise. Truly magic when you're not really in a hurry. Might as well have that second cup of coffee if you have the firewood.

It would be easy to stay and chill out but we got to do some miles today.

Things are easy. Well almost. Every major road junction or town has a security check point but there is no real hassle. But sure as eggs is eggs we get stopped at every one of them. Hey! we stand out a bit.

Never just the one check. Our passports are always past around for all to see but today he asks me if I have pen. Eh no (not if your gonna write in me passport I've not)! He asks Heidi and she says no. Thankfully remembering the story of the last twat to write in her passport. WTF was he gonna write? Idiot!..

Just glad Heidi was on the same page. He gave us them back when we weren't forth coming with a pen.

Food, fuel and out of town. Across the Nile to the Nubian Desert. Not much to really see along the way in terms of monuments and stuff but the scenery is just gob-smackingly awesome. I'm glad that there is very little in the way of villages or even the odd house to be honest, but there were a few. Enough to make the place look lived in, just about.

Besides, watching the desert flow as it does was more calming than most of the roads that Africa had thrown at us.

We rode for hours with nothing but our own thoughts it seemed. Stopping to take pics and a little video here and there. It coincided with the gathering of the sticks & twigs for cooking.

Off the road for the day, we had done enough. A good spot out in the rocks with the now essential sand base for the tent. Things starting to hurt, what with the duff sleeping mattress.

There was a few goats around so there must be people and sure enough, man on donkey rides by looking for them. It's that time of day. Collect what needs protecting before nightfall. He waves at us and goes about his business.

We sit amongst the rocks watching the sunset once more. Cuppa in hand with a full stomach… A man could get used to this!

Watching the stars appear once more. Don't believe I've ever been so aware of the moon state before. I know what size it's gonna be most nights along with it's rise & fall never mind which direction to look. Sweet dreams…

Up with the new day and a steady start once more. Off to see the pyramids of Nuri. They're a bit on the ruined side but you can imagine how things used to be. Much softer sandstone I guess and they've not weathered well.

Bumped into a Czech couple. Embassy Diplomat with his wife and guide in tow. Nice chat. The guardians turn up to ask for the visitors fee and travel pass which was good timing. Translator at hand. He turns and asks us if we're the newlyweds? Oh em!

[Video No. 49: **Nubian Dessert**]

Shady from the other day has phoned here as well. We get charged local price once more.

In that case we're the newlyweds!:-) got used to calling ourselves husband & wife. Nice thought but Heidis not one for marriage. Our plan to set up home together in Bulgaria is growing arms and legs and that will do for now.

Across the river. Hey! cyclist. Quick turnaround for a chat and maybe some info. John an Englishman and Boon from Korea. They had teamed up to cross the desert sections as they were both traveling in roughly the same direct. South. Even if they were chalk and cheese.

Good to have friends on the road at times.

Bypass the local pyramids and museum at Jebel Barkel in favour of some late lunch, before heading out into the desert proper once more. Unbelievably the road ran straight by the pyramids…

Scenes of the night before but no one around and no wildlife. The stars and the moon are the same though. Well almost, just the timings have advanced.

There definitely something very peaceful out here. Almost no distractions form what is the true beauty of the Desert.

[Video No. 50: **WooPee**]

Rest Day Dongola

Think the traveling is catching up with us if I'm honest. Rest days are never long enough. With washing your kit and bike maintenance to catch up on they went by in a flash… Hey it all needed done.

But it was good to get going again.

Dafoofa. The oldest mud brick built town in Africa

A tall claim but one that is gathering momentum as the archaeologists uncover more of the site.

But finding the site wasn't easy. So we stopped to ask directions. Which was easy enough. But you must eat with us. Come, come.

Mohammed and his family were fantastic hosts. Lunch was simple foul and omelette but excellent as was the conversation. He had good English to.

After being interrogated over lunch the younger brother had the task of showing us the way. Glad he did too. A few back alleys had to be negotiated to get there.

But worth the effort. The great Defoofa was the oldest mud built building in Africa. Not much recognisable but a massive erection in itself. Just Awesome. The early pieces of township in the making. The museum was worth the look too. Revelations of a bygone era

But onward we must go. We hit the road.

Not enough time to do any distance to a town of any consequence which suited us. Another night in the desert please. Take them when you can was our thinking, you don't know when you'll be able to from now on.

A chance meeting with a German cyclist. A tour guide researching his route for his next tour. Luxor to Khartoum. We chatted about all sorts. The trauma of Ethiopia included as we couldn't imagine being a cyclist there. He agreed with gusto. Not his idea of fun.

Said our farewells and went in search of that night's campsite.

Easy enough but more and more activity around. More and more people too. Strange as there wasn't that much in the way of villages along the way.

Stopped in a quiet spot and carried out our well-rehearsed routine. Clear our pitch and cook. Watch the sunset with our cup o' tea. Can't say fairer than that.

Mosque and the call to prayer in the distance accompanied with the sound of a generator carried by the wind. Mmm… village can't be that far away then. But a peaceful night once more.

Strange village. More like some sort of road camp. But no road being built. Lots of rocks being crushed and earth movements but nothing being built. Mmm…

Abri and a short day. Time to rest in the only guesthouse. Gather our thoughts before border Day. A chance to go site seeing too.

An old Moggy (Morris Minor) sitting outside. Awesome nic for it's age. No salt corrosion here I suppose. Issued to the diplomatic service out here back in the day maybe.

[Video No. 51: **Moggys Big Day Out**]

Mahmoud was a great guy. Showed us around the local temple and took us to his friend's house. All very traditional and great company. Mostly women at home but conversation and kindness a plenty. Happy days.

Up early the following day and of on a boat trip to Si Island. History for all to see. Left to wonder amongst the ruins on our own.

Lunch and a hubble bubble smoke with the locals. Not smoked in years but while in Rome and all that. They told us of the gold panning out in the desert which explained a few things. The road camps from the days before. A bit of money changing on the side and we're happy to get going.

Off to Wadi Halfa and the Egyptian border. What might be our last night camping out in the desert.

Not that I slept much as this was the border I'd been dreading from the outset.

I'd been to Egypt many years ago and hated almost every minute of it.

Shithole is the only way I could describe it. I made jokes about the Pharaohs being buried with their entourage. Whatever and whoever was left was the slaves, not the creators of one of the worlds greatest civilisations.

Before their time, so why was the country in such a mess.

Shithole...

Yip! I never gave them any good press that's for sure.

Sleepless... to say the least... but another night out under the stars. Wild dogs to keep my attention focused. They didn't bother us really but there were plenty of paw prints around in the morning for sure. Little else but the odd truck or car driving by on the other side of our hill... But you can't put it off forever. We had an appointment at one of Africa's most notorious border crossings...

Not many kilometres down the road we run into the back of the cue. Cue of trucks that is. Won't be waiting in that one though.

Up the front and everyone is cool with it as they're all truckers on a different schedule it seems. Customs for them will be intrusive and time consuming me thinks. But before we even went anywhere a trucker say we must speak with Kamal.

Really!

You find him he'll help. In fact, here! I'll phone him.

Before we knew it we were being helped whither we wanted it or not. I had heard of this guy from various travel forums but Heidi wanted to try it for herself. I just wanted the easy life. But Kamal just seemed to take over. All in a good way. A real nice guy.

It was easy... For him that is...

Less than a couple of hours and we were out. Yeah it was as easy as that... Result!

Hi Honey

Now the tricky bit. Getting into Egypt

Out came the paper notice of offices to go to. The 1st border crossing point I've ever had to pay to get into. My head goes down just imagining what's to come.

Shock horror and more shock.

Off Heidi goes as I've got the bikes. She's back within minutes. There's a men only and a female only queuing system. Result she's sent to the front.

I'll be sitting with the bikes then...

Plenty of attention as usual even the police chief himself. Honey he said. Well honey this is Heidi. I then told him about how people show affection for each other call one and other honey back home. He just laughs. A larger than life character who ran the show around here. He wished us well.

An almost brand new border crossing with a definite system. Still too much paperwork but before I knew it I was sitting outside the police chief's office putting on my Egyptian number plates. Woohoo...

Off to find the ferry to Abu Simbel. Off to Find somewhere to stay the night.

Desert and not much else but we had to keep rolling. late afternoon for the last ferry as it doesn't run during the night time hours. just no need if the border crossing isn't open. Strictly a daytime routine.

There's a few abandoned buildings here and there. Small farms and homesteads clinging to the waters edge. How close they came to being flooded out as the waters rose in years gone by? Mmm… But there's no time to hang around, or so we thought.

Join the cue at the ferry on/off ramp. There's a dozen trucks but they're not all getting on. It's just a little RoRo with room for half a dozen trucks or so.

Chance for a photo-shoot with the truckers while we're waiting. Well when I say photo-shoot. What I really mean is the Blonde Haired White Lady with all the truckers. More FaceBook Boyfriends me thinks! I really wish I could see those pages. Makes me wonder what they say…

We're sent to the front of the cue when it's time to board. There's always room for a little one. Me thinks the truckers are sleeping at the lakeside.

A cool boat ride to be honest. Friendly folks all happy to see us. More photos and plenty kids coming to practice their English on us.

Abu Simbel came all so quickly.

Toyu guest house was more expensive than we normally would pay but they did say comeback if we didn't find a better deal. It didn't take long to find out we wouldn't.

Hey! a few days and nights of luxury would be good for us and it was Heidis birthday and she deserved a treat after her border crossing expertise. Shaking her hair and batting her eyelids more like. But she uses her womanly ways on me most days and it always works.

Remember? If you Loved Me! Happy Days!:-)

31

The Upper & Lower Kingdoms

Ramises II

Easy days of rest and a Wi-Fi catch-up. The start of our last country in Africa but we found ourselves trying to sort out life for when we got back home. Between that and the shipping of our bikes to Europe we fired emails in all directions.

Bikes on a ship to Greece. Flights to Athens. Heidi has a contract for the summer. I get an invite for an interview. It's all go!go!go!

It did feel good and make the sitting square wheeled feel a whole lot better.

Some site seeing. Some of the monuments that were moved when the dam at Aswan was built. As the water rose UNESCO worked furiously moving as many of the great monuments that the Pharaohs left us. They would have been lost to the rising waters otherwise.

That didn't prepare us for what we found. When the phrase "monumental" is banded around people use it out of context. These were colossal works of art really and if no one explained how they were moved, you would be impressed. The fact is, that they did move them to the current location was a truly monumental task of the new era.

You're amazed by this feat of modern day engineering then when you accept it, you can absorb the greatness of the work of the ancients that stand before you.

Monumental Task. Monumental Egypt.

More chat with the locals. A bit of money changing. Fill up the bikes (20 cents per ltr). Something for lunch and hit the road.

300km to Aswan a journey that took 3 days on the old ferry. Glad we could ride the road as I've heard the tales of that border crossing and ferry journey of old. Didn't fancy that one if I'm honest.

Aswan came easy. Even if it was a 300km journey. Something that's not the norm for us.

Not much traffic on the road. Just a few check points and the odd coffee shack. I was expecting the security detail and convoy system. Things must be more stable than they have been. For sure they've not been the best since the revolution. The tourists have stayed away due to the instability and threat from terrorism.

Everyone was cool with us but they did stress the Nubian Card though. Something they were proud of. Southern Egypt and northern Sudan (Nubian Desert) the southern kingdom of old.

A few days in Aswan

Quite cool. Great food to be had everywhere, friendly people too. The hotel wasn't the Toya but they were friendly enough. It wasn't easy to find somewhere safe for the bikes. So we opted for the pedestrian lane that ran by the hotel reception. It was manned all night so all was good.

The longer you stay somewhere the better it gets. Return to the same street cafe for coffee each morning and they get to know you. Return to the same cafe for food. They get to know you too. That night time cup o' tea, we'll pick yet another street cafe. Even returning to your favourite pastry shop got you noticed. Yeah it was a routine but the locals all treated us better for it I'm sure. Your coffee was always close at hand as was you cup of tea. As for your meals, well they were always good and we were the only ones that were given cutlery. Think they saw how useless I was eating with bread in hand.

1st Cataract

Aswan was as far as you could sail up the Nile. So diverse a place as you find in Egypt. Monuments Tombs and Shrines a plenty. Many of Egypt's monuments were quarried from here. The site of the unfinished obelisk filled in many the blanks for archaeologist and one that made you wonder what life was really like at the time. Well cool.

Think that's what Africa has done for me. Made me think of its troubled past. It's transformations. It's wonders!

It felt like Egypt was bringing it to a new high. Gob-Smacked really and it just keeps on coming.

Numerous sites around the country. Some one hundred and eighty pyramids and new ones being discovered almost daily it seemed. More statues being dug up even as we travelled through. Mind blowing.

To think that so much of this once great empire's treasures were forgotten and lost to the desert is probably the most mind blowing of all. Some buried intentionally and others simply swallowed by the deserts shifting sands.

On to Luxor and the site if some of the grandest of sites along the Nile.

We hit the campsite. Well, Hotel really as there was not real chance of camping to be honest. But we were glad of the room, excellent food and a base to go site seeing from. Hey! we could walk to most of them.

It was said that at the time of antiquity development, these temples were just a part of the village and village life carried on in and around the broken remnants of this great site.

The restoration work was impressive enough for me. The untrained eye was truly amazed at what lay before me. Loved every bit of it...

Arnak must be the most impressive I've seen. Colossal columns and endless sphinx figure along its avenue just blew me away. Walking around with me mouth open trying to make sense of it all. Good days.

[Video No. 52: **Egypty**]

More of a mixture here and not so much of the Nubian influences. Things are a changing. More of a hustle on the street but not bad really. Mmm… this is the Egypt I remember. Well at least some of it. We're bad tourists though. Just no chance of selling us any of your gizzets or tat. But I was susceptible to walking like an Egyptian it seems. Straight to that newest of worshiping temples… The toilet!!!

A couple of days in bed as I was drained. Just needed to sit it out but there wasn't enough time left to take it to easy. Last chance to visit the Valley of the Kings. So we took it. Another great one. Struggled a bit to take it all in though.

Fellow Sinners. WhatAShitHole…

Yip! it's fair to say I've bad mouthed Egypt in the past. It's been 20 years but Honestly! I didn't have a good time. This time around I was dreading it.

That was then and this is now. Since the border it's been really cool. The Temples of Abu Simbel, Aswan and Luxor. The penny has finally dropped. The Pharaohs built them to pay homage to the gods thanking them for victory in battle while cleansing there sole.

Modern day Egypt is just about the same. But their new temples are only built for one. Smooth porcelain and cool ceramics. Just assume the position and pay homage.

Hey! my sole is fully cleansed.

But Egypt has not really changed…

Oops maybe I'm not fully cleansed…

32
Going the distance

We had to push on to meet up with a ship to Europe. God only knows what the paperwork for customs will be like.

If that was to have been our only worry then it would have been fine with me.

Just as you get on the road and a sparkle in your eye it all goes Pete Tong!

We get stopped at a police check point close to the edge of town.

You have to be escorted. Mmm… ok… And that was that. The next three days were absolute hell.

We weren't allowed any freedom whatsoever. When we went to the ancient sites we were the only people to have our luggage searched and I.D. checked. Passports, driving license and all sorts of questions. I was beginning to wonder if it was for our safety or we weren't to be trusted. Maybe it was us that was the threat to their national security. I think it gripped me more as they were so unprofessional at their job.

They never checked anyone else apart from us. WTF?

If they got hit by terrorist it's their own fault for being so shit at their job…

A bit harsh! No one deserves to be hit by anyone. Just frustrating…

We were handed from security detail to security detail with hardly a word exchanged with us. No idea what was going on half the time? Neither did they I suppose.

Taken to hotels we just wouldn't have chosen in a month of Sundays, and never a moment's peace. No stops for food drink or even the toilet.

It stretched us for sure. Heidi had a meltdown as it seemed to be taking forever. We were in danger of missing our boat at this rate.

Things speeded up but then no stops of any kind. Feck that, we're off for lunch. Well not quite that way.

We had another melt down, this time at each other. That wasn't fair on either us. Just a sign of the situation but we stopped for lunch without them.

It didn't last long as we were picked up as we left town. Too good to be true eh!

Thankfully on our third day, the outskirts of Cairo where approaching. Just as easy as we were picked up, we were let go. Freedom!

We stopped out of sight of the checkpoint. Coke? Hell yeah!

Sat with a group of local lads for 20 mins wondering what all the fuss was about.

Hey! off up the road to the impromptu campsite. Maryanne Stroud Gabanni.

Great woman, Great place to stay even if the pack of dogs scared the shit out of me...

How often do you see 2 Great Danes in the same garden not to mention the rest of them... must have been a dozen of all shapes and sizes.

She gave us a place to camp, shower and just relax in her inpromtu campsite. She probably never really knew how much we needed to just chill. Her company and her food were more than enough to put a smile back on our faces. Wonderful women...

Even had a day to go site seeing.

Saqqara

We thought we'd crack Saqqara and the Great Pyramids in a day. They weren't far apart... How wrong can you be?

Driving license… sounded like a statement not a request to see it.

Really? It's a tourist site. What do you want to see that for?

You're not allowed in with the motorbike.

Well what do you want to see my driving license for?

We showed him it anyways, and at that he demands to check our bags. Which would be fine if he had gone through the bus load of tourist the other fuckwit had just waved through.

You not gonna check the bus?

Why are you giving us the special treatment?

It's not me. The Antiquities Department says so.

You mean the Antiquities Department make you treat all tourists this way? Or are we special?

Please Carry on. You can go through now and welcome.

Hey I don't feel very welcome!

Strange look comes back at me but it's true. I've never felt less welcome throughout Africa.

The site was amazing but the walking back and forth was hell in our physical condition. More of the games to get money out of tourists. The backsheesh! I'm not immune to it by any means but the shutters are up.

I'll give you a tip. Let me in on my bike next time…

The underground chamber, Serapeum of Saqqara eased the pain. Something which was different to what we had seen anywhere else along the Nile. An endless corridor tomb with off shoots which housed the great granite sarcophagus. Originally filled with a dead bull. Yip! you heard me. Something to do with the belief that they became immortal after their death. Who am I to mock someone else beliefs… Santa's real right?

All broken into or lids removed but something to behold that's for sure, and for once it was ok to bribe to guardian. We were supposed to buy an extra ticket to gain entrance to the tomb. But we had none. Not the first time he's let someone in and pocketed the money I'll bet. It saved us the 2km walk back to the ticket booth so didn't feel guilty about it. Hey! we were the only people walking the trails in between sites. Was glad to stick two fingers up to the jobsworth twat at the gate… Welcome indeed…

[Video No. 53: **Cow coffin**]

Stop for lunch. A set menu but one I could live with. We have beer too. Yip! Could do with one of those… Not on the top of our game yet   but It's worth the risk!

Lunch was a fixed price. Tourist price but fixed none the less. Always ask upfront. Which we did. The beer was a bonus but at what price. Bugga we didn't ask. When the bill came it was twice the price of the last one we had bought at the hotel in Luxor. Which was tourist price.

Thieving twat! And you wonder why there is so little tourists? I hope you can get a job farming cause you're not gonna have any tourists for much longer. Always! But Always! ask the price first!!! Here endith the lesson!

They're all chancers and just can't help it…. This is more like the Egypt I can remember but shouldn't get too annoyed. You just can't stay pissed off forever

Back to Maryanne's and the sanctuary that her farm provided. Maryanne was a fearsome women on her day. Remember the strong African women. Well she went that bit further. A Canadian national born in California who moved to the very edge of town to start her farm, leaving the comforts of the city behind. Horses, cows, goats and an awesome vegetable patch.

One strong lady in a very male dominated country. I laughed as she tells me the story of sacking all of her farm labourers and starting over. She was definitely the boss. Did I say before? A wonderful woman…

[Video No. 54: **Last Ride**]

No time really for the great pyramids but we will drive by and see if there is a picture to be had. Not really, but we do get to see them amongst the haze of the morning.

I'd seen them before and to be honest wasn't that interested. More impressive from the roadside. Not much to see inside. Heidi opted for the we'll catch them on the way back approach as we have to fly back to Europe out of Cairo.

So it's the fast moving desert road to Alexandria.

Not very inspiring nor scenic if it be told. Just a means to an end. Alexandria and the end of the road. It all came on us pretty quick. It seemed like no time at all and we were working our way through the traffic heading for the Colonnade and the Mediterranean Sea. Twisted this way and that with the one-way system I can't believe it spat us out right in front of the Old Cecil Hotel, couldn't pick a better spot. Just awesome. Not that we could afford a room in there but still pretty cool. The thought of the place being filled by the British GCHQ of its day during the war.

Heidi had a quick look for a cheeky hotel with parking. That would be the stumbling block. Hey! a few minutes later fixer in tow she had found one.

Glad to give him a few quid. Headache averted finding a safe place for the bikes. It was cheap and cheerful but when Heidi opened up the balcony doors everything else was forgotten. What stretched out before us was a sight for sore eyes. The Mediterranean Sea.

What A Ride! :-)

[Video No. 55: **Last call Alexandria**]

Slap up Pizza and a bottle or two of wine to celebrate. Alexandria wasn't the town I could remember...

Hopefully the shipping company would deal with the rest. For a price as always...

It didn't matter what lay before us, for now a cuddle up together for Going The Distance... it's off to dreamland...

33
Dreamland

Sitting in Athens

Waiting on our bikes to turn up in Athens, it just seemed to take an age. Delays, day after day... Rough seas apparently, but it did give us time to do the tourist thing. A city tour with a local historian from the university. A wealth of information and full of ideas of what's what. She gave us many an idea for visiting the sights that were a must around town.

Pointed in the direction of the Acropolis, we scrambled over the rocky outcrops on route to the heavens. Still wheezing a bit but it was worth the effort as the view of the city was tremendous. You really could appreciate just why it was built up there. A steady pace required for the exploration of this once great citadel. Ok! I really was wheezing like a wheezy thing.

An easier pace at the newly built Acropolis Museum. Something that our wheeziness could cope with. You did have to use your imagination as almost everything is vandalised or broken. Ok, vandalised from the sacking of the city by the Venetians back in the day. However broken it was it still had a story to tell.

We continued that easy pace around the old city market place. All cool and a real reminder that we were back in Europe. I think I've mentioned before when travelling through Africa, that market day was the life and soul of a village or community. Even in the bigger towns and cities they were a buzz and the life blood to all.

Here in Athens there just wasn't that same hustle and bustle. Very civilised, just not Africa. Walking the streets Heidis flipflops gave way. We were all flip and no flop. Leather sandals on sale everywhere but we walked/shuffled for a bit in search of super glue. I think we both looked at each other for a moment. Africa had taken its toll on us and all our possessions. Back in Africa no one would have batted an eyelid in our direction. Here? There was looks of judgment, a real difference and we were the ones in desperate need of restoration...

We did enjoy the next week or so traveling north to The MotoKamp and Bulgaria. Sunshine, beach, mountains and monasteries, even had time for a visit to the Devils Throat Gorge where it had all went oh so horribly wrong for Heidis bike some eighteen months before. Cold and snowing in on us along the way. It was great to get to Idilevo and meet old friends. They made us feel right at home as that's what I thought it was gonna be. Home!

We did spend some time house hunting. Even put in a cheeky wee offer in on one. A house in Bulgaria and all that it would entail. Excited? Hell Yeah! And if life was perfect then I'm sure we would have worked it all out. Our long distance relationship had gone its distance.

Blighty

A flight home to Blighty as it's just too cold to cross Europe and the Alps in our African riding gear. The ride into Bulgaria had told us that one, but home we soon were.

Good to be at Heidis parents' home with them. Well-fed and well looked after. They had looked out for us on more than one occasion when we were away and it was great to share a few stories across the table with them.

A chance to start that fitness thing we had been talking about. Hiking and cycling was on the cards but as always there's a hiccup. Two years on the motorbike had taken its toll on us and me more than Heidi.

Two days into cycling told me something wasn't right. Jimmys back was just not what it used to be.

Some sort of muscle issue. Maybe it was The Old Guy thing I don't know. I'd have to get someone to check it out. But as we discussed what's possible and what's not for the next few weeks, one thing was clear. Jimmy couldn't cycle! Hell it felt like I'd been stabbed in the back!

We did go visiting Heidis family, oh hiking and biking too. Jimmy taking up his time to go running and nunchucks while Heidi went off and did her own thing on her mountain bike. I'm not a cripple, I Just can't sit on a bicycle and pull on the bars.

Heidi has plans for competing in the Iditarod, a long distance bike race across Alaska. Maybe I should leave her to get on with her training. But I'm all at sixes and sevens. Don't know why? Just feel strange leaving Heidi after being with each other night and day for so long. Just Strange… Our lives seem to be going in different directions.

Home wasn't much better. Crashing at my sisters flat, I didn't really want to go out and meet people. I did but only on a few occasions. Not overwhelmed by it all surely? Just felt strange, wanted to hide away. Missing the road I guess for there I loved meeting new faces. Spent the next few weeks trying to make sense of it all.

Not what we had dreamt of over the last few years but back in Blighty our lives were in very different places. We decided to go our separate ways. Granted we both love travel and maybe it was easy to dream of pastures new. It's all so easy in Dreamland but I think in the cold light of day we are very different people. Maybe it was time to follow our own dreams…

My sister convinced me to go to the Isle of Man for the TT as I had originally planned. This was where it had all began some two years before. The first place Heidi and I had gone when we gave up work. My mate Jock was cool with it all as I'm always welcome. Brothers in arms kinda thing. Glad he looked out for me. Miserable Bastard. Sorry I spoiled his TT for him. Emotional fuckup me thinks.

Happy Home Coming

It's fair to say coming home wasn't what I thought it was gonna be. It should have been relaxing and refreshing, battery recharge and throw yourself forward into whatever the future holds. Mmm.

Yeah! the anxiety which accompanied my home coming didn't come alone. The Danakil Lurgi which lay under the surface for months, came to the surface and took the lime light. I've been drained and out of breath for so long. Thought it was the result of two years sitting on my bike to be honest. So Unfit! My Emotional State! The hiking and cycling routine had faltered along with the rest of life it seemed. But it was a little bit more than that.

Schistosomiasis (bilharzia) a water borne parasite described as Snail Fever sometimes giving you the swimmers itch. You don't have to swallow this one. It bores its way through the skin and into your blood stream. Different strains affecting you in different ways. A fresh-water snail which can have a long term effect on you if left untreated. Wow this just might explain a few things...

The Manx Health Service testing my blood, poo and wee for the little devils, not to mention sending me for chest X-rays looking for Tuberculosis. That one scared me for a bit. Bugga! I spent days reading up on it and trying to work out in my mind where I could have come in contact with it.

Thinking back the first time I felt so out of breath was Addis Ababa, Ethiopia... Oh! the itch thing that I thought was animal fleas when we went hiking in the Bale Mountains... We had been swimming in Lake Turkana only days before... All was slowly falling into place...

As I read more it seems to be more common place than you think. In fact it was a common cause of death for Egyptians in the Greco-Roman time. The blood in the urine thought to be Male Menstruation as it was in such common place in teenage years. So common that there is reports of parents bringing teenage boys to be seen by the doctor when the flow did not come. That journey into manhood eh... Mmm...

The Manx Health Service was good enough to send to Germany for medication to sort me out. Just wish they could have sorted out my head. It seems to be taking time that one. A broken man me thinks. I still am in many ways, but When The Road Throws You a Curved One and all that... Slap a Knee Down on It... Just get out and Ride...

I did go and pick up Jack Sparrow from our friends at the MotoKamp in Bulgaria and took to the road. A quick one for a change. The direct route to Switzerland as close friends of mine were getting married.

It was great to chat with Dom and Susanne after sitting on the IOM with my own thoughts (We're all too good at over thinking things and if you're not careful, your demons will come get you). I went back to school, well Dom invited me to chat to his 15 and 16 year old Swiss English students. I have no idea what they really thought of my Scottish accent. But I did enjoy their company.

The students were in school oh so early (seven o'clock) and they had a two way interaction with their teacher. Submitting a request for help on topics which they were struggling with, and he'd sort work out for the following week. Could do with some of that myself. A truly refreshing attitude for life and learning. Talking with them made me open up, recalling all the things I loved about traveling. Yeah, I'm no teenager any more but they helped me more than they would ever know.

After the wedding I wrote to Hieke at Horizons Unlimited in Switzerland. They were having an Overland Travellers meeting and I offered to present some of my story to them. Talking to the kids at school had done exactly that. Got me talking again. The schedule was full but Hieke said she would squeeze me in.

Fellow travellers and we all love a good story! Sorted out some pictures, videos and gave the presentation I should have given back in the UK when we had first got home.

Some inspirational presenters and like-minded travellers. Great chat with, and advice from Ted Simon the true grandfather of motorcycle adventure travel. Told some stories and with the help of my new friends all was good with the world. Well almost... Just talking it all through made me realise some things... Ok not the meaning of life but things that were on my mind...

When I had returned from a previous long distance road trip I found myself at home and back into the same old routine all too quickly. I hadn't planned for coming home and how my life may change. I fell back into that same old over-worked routine. I slipped back into the clutches of the Rat Race I'd been trying to escape... I had just not thought it through.

I could remember taking to Danny the South African biker we had met way back in Zimbabwe. He was questioning how travelling would change him. My advice to him back then was to have a plan for when he returned home. Have direction, have focus, you don't have to be regimented about it, but have at least one idea for your next trip. Didn't have to be a long trip just something to look forward to.

I didn't really have any back then! Direction that is. Just focused on work when I returned from that last journey and it didn't really work for me... This time I did have plans, new house, new work direction new focus for future life... they were just not that realistic... Dreamland's got a lot to answer for eh!

Picking up Jack Sparrow from Bulgaria and meeting up with friends in Switzerland gave me another chance of going home, to come up with a plan of attack for my future. It at least gave me the focus to finish telling my story and putting it down on paper for you. The slow road home to the Isle of Man with peace to work it all out.

It was a lonely road at times but easy on my mind. Time to think! I needed Road Tax and a MOT for the little bike when I got to Dover. Straight off the ferry and the guys at the test station were full of questions and admiration for the little bike. Nearly two and a half years, thirty-four different countries and nearly 60,000 km, (Yeah! Sixty Thousand Kilometres) since his last MoT. All that Jack Sparrow needed was a Stop&Tale light bulb and a stick-on reflector for the number plate and all was good...

Jack Sparrow won't let you down… What A Ride!

I am smart enough to know that there is three sides to every story, and I'm sure Heidi would have seen our journey so very differently through her eyes. But in my madness this just happens to be mine… Just glad we managed to go the distance.

Would I do it again?

Bugga back In Mongolia when it was all going Pete Tong for me and my Tiger a friend of mine simply said, "If nothing ever went wrong! Your stories just wouldn't be that interesting. You can buy a package holiday tour to almost anywhere." Reading through these words it seems like I've picked out all the things that's gone wrong throughout the journey. Hey! it could have been worse but I'm sure I just wouldn't have had it any other way and there was a thousand wonderful stories in-between.

Sure, I've been lucky enough to travel to lots of places in my life, just didn't think I'd had ever gone back to Africa after my early Egyptian experience. So for that I do thank Heidi.

A few years ago I was chewing the fat and having a laugh with a guy at the HuBB UK meet at Donnington.

Does Yir Arse fit Yi, in your best Scottish accent said at speed became, Zdrastvooyte (dras-feet-chya) Russian for hello. I laughed many a time when I said it whilst traveling through Russia that summer. It turned in my head to does your arse actually fit you.

Does this traveling life suit you? It doesn't suit everyone.

I'm still dreaming… and where would you rather be?